PERSEVERANCE
HOW TO DEVELOP IT

THE TEN TITLES IN THE

MENTAL EFFICIENCY SERIES

∾

POISE: HOW TO ATTAIN IT
  D. STARKE
CHARACTER: HOW TO STRENGTHEN IT
  D. STARKE
TIMIDITY: HOW TO OVERCOME IT
  YORITOMO-TASHI
INFLUENCE: HOW TO EXERT IT
  YORITOMO-TASHI
COMMON SENSE: HOW TO EXERCISE IT
  YORITOMO-TASHI
PRACTICALITY: HOW TO ACQUIRE IT
  R. NICOLLE
OPPORTUNITIES: HOW TO MAKE THE
  MOST OF THEM
  L. CHARLEY
PERSEVERANCE: HOW TO DEVELOP IT
  H. BESSER
SPEECH: HOW TO USE IT
    EFFECTIVELY
  XANTHES
PERSONALITY: HOW TO BUILD IT
  H. LAURENT

∾

FUNK & WAGNALLS COMPANY
Publishers
NEW YORK AND LONDON

MENTAL EFFICIENCY SERIES

PERSEVERANCE
HOW TO DEVELOP IT

By H. BESSER

TRANSLATED BY FRANCIS MEDHURST, D.LITT.

AUTHORIZED EDITION

"Success attends him who determines to persevere."

PUBLISHED BY BROWNSTONE BOOKS

PREFACE

OF all the modern "Keys to Fortune" none more easily turns the tumblers of the lock of Life than Perseverance. This quality Plutarch described as all-powerful. Said he, "Perseverance is the best friend and ally of those who use properly the opportunities that it presents, and the worst enemy of those who rush into action before it summons them."

With his motto "Success attends him who determines to persevere," the Author of this work describes true perseverance; points out the impediments to its attainment and the obstacles to be overcome. The Reader is warned against the dangers of that excessive enthusiasm which leads to precipitancy, and is urged, above all things, never to be precipitate, for precipitancy is the handmaiden of error and the companion of misfortune. Likewise, he is advised to eschew obstinacy as the companion of ignorance, self-conceit, and false pride. Obstinacy is an indication of a weak judgment and a stubborn mind. The obstinate man is wanting in culture, for he lacks both delicacy and refinement of temper.

Edmund Burke described obstinacy as a great vice which was frequently the cause of great mischief, for it is allied to constancy, fortitude, fidelity, firmness, and magnanimity—all commendable virtues, which if practised to excess lead to obstinacy, the one passion that never recovers from failure. It is the pathway to that narrowness of mind which leads to self-conceit.

Perseverance is the dogged determination that overcomes difficulties which appear insurmountable. "Victory," said the great Napoleon, "belongs to him who has the most perseverance." The spirit of indomitable perseverance crowns every worthy effort. Here is a simple but effective guide to this great power.

The Second Part of this work is devoted by the Author to teaching how to acquire that moral force which leads to the development of Perseverance. By practical exercises he points out the way to secure it; teaches the control of self through the influence of the will, and leads the diffident man to self-reliance and that perseverance which plucks success even from the spear-point. The battle-cry of all who would succeed must be "Perseverance," but this battle-cry, like all others, is worthless without support.

By Perseverance Hannibal crossed the Alps in fifteen days, Julius Cæsar in eleven, and Napoleon the Great in five. He that would attain success must support it with persistent effort full worthy of his aim; for, just as the Indian strikes fire as the reward of continuous endeavor, so can we achieve success by indomitable and unceasing exertion, and thus, on the forge of experience, model the Key that shall turn the lock of Life and open the doors to Fortune.

Every earnest Reader of the following pages may draw from them that strength of mind, clearness of thought, and force of character that awaken enthusiasm, and inspire that confidence which the world at large readily grants to the persevering and successful man.

THE PUBLISHERS.

CONTENTS

viii CONTENTS

PART I

THE IMPEDIMENTS TO
PERSEVERANCE

CHAPTER I

TRUE PERSEVERANCE

PERSEVERANCE is that faculty which gives us the power to accomplish a piece of work without allowing ourselves to be turned aside from our purpose either by the initial difficulties involved or by the obstacles that multiply themselves as we progress with our task.

It is that form of energy which enables us to develop sufficient strength of will never to be discouraged by the labor we have to face in accomplishing what we set out to do.

It is the art of marching directly forward toward the goal we have set before us, quite ignoring all temporary embarrassments, great or small, save by putting forth all our strength to surmount them.

It is the quality found in people of an enthusiastic temperament, who, once they have discerned the favorable possibilities of an enterprise, allow nothing to divert them and can never be defeated by the occurrences that tend to hinder its successful outcome.

11

The people who possess perseverance are of
the type that is able to keep walking steadily
in the path that has been chosen, despite the
pitfalls encountered along the way.

Obstacles, far from lessening the courage of
such people, seem rather to redouble it.

The fever of battle increases their strength
tenfold and the difficulties they meet merely
sharpen their wits.

The persevering know nothing of the weaknesses which serve to defeat those whose feeble
wills go to pieces at the first encounter with
opposing forces.

Such people abandon themselves to despair
and cast all the blame upon fate, which has
nothing to do with it.

They are very careful not to admit their own
incompetence and make no attempt to change it
into the energy that will accomplish results.

Their ineptitude is much better suited to inaction and they cease to struggle toward the
goal while excusing themselves to their own
consciences by exclaiming:

"Nothing succeeds with me! It is much
wiser to persevere no longer!"

All the same they miss no opportunity of
expatiating upon the luck of their neighbors

who are able to carry all their undertakings to
a successful issue.

"Oh! If that were I," they cry, "it wouldn't
come out in that way! For them everything
goes right!"

Their envy has led them to state a truth.

Practically speaking, everything succeeds for
the man who has will-power and perseverance
and nothing can ever come to a successful ter-
mination in the hands of the man who deliberately ignores his opportunities of making every
favorable slant of fortune serve his purpose.

Never at any period in the world's history was
perseverance more necessary than it is in our
social conditions of the present day.

The spread of general education, in quicken-
ing so many talents that were formerly merely
dormant in the germ, has enormously increased
the number of competitors in the struggle.

The battle has become for this reason much
more bitter and more long-drawn out, and demands of those who are engaged in it an inflex-
ible will, backed up by untiring effort, which is
the base of all perseverance.

This persistence of purpose does not merely
bring into play the qualities needed to hasten
the accomplishment of an end we have in view.

It is also the result of an idea that has been pondered over and cherished in the mind until such time as it has acquired sufficient vitality to be able to transform itself into deeds.

It will remain sterile if the goal is not clearly visioned. Before we are able to maintain our course with tenacity in one fixt path it is indispensable that we must know exactly where it leads.

The number of those who wander along blind alleys is legion. These people are filled with astonishment when they encounter difficulties that it was given to them to foresee, if they would. Those who are endowed with perseverance collect their forces at this stage; they reflect upon the nature of the obstacles they are likely to encounter and estimate their own forces of resistance.

If they feel themselves unable to make headway against the barriers before them; if they foresee that these difficulties will very surely soon become impossibilities, they will not hesitate a moment, but will go back to their starting-point and will look for a more practical route.

Nevertheless, for many people to abandon a project is to convince themselves of their own weakness, and they will shrink from a determination which appears to them in the light of a failure.

But for the man of energy the obstacles are the enemy, and, just as a soldier would think himself dishonored were he to fly in the face of a movement of the hostile forces, he will feel himself lowered in his own estimation if he does not keep up the struggle to the very end.

The first thing to be done by those who find themselves in this position of difficulty is to stop marching forward, not in order to retire, at first, but to give themselves time for reflection.

We shall see later on that it is vitally necessary never to do anything without consideration if one has made up one's mind to be persevering.

Reasoning should be the foundation of all our enterprises.

The man who engages in a fight without first having decided that such a step was necessary is beaten before he starts.

What soldier would think of going to war without his weapons?

In the struggle for life the battle is no less bitter than on the field of carnage and it is sometimes equally deadly.

When one is sufficiently informed upon the

efforts that must be put forth, and when one has reflected in advance upon the windings and the difficulties of the road ahead, it will be time to take up the question of shortening the first and of surmounting the second.

The parent of all perseverance is the power of the motive idea.

This virtue has been much calumniated.

The weaklings and the incapable are glad to give it the name of "mania" or "fixt idea."

But fixity of ideas is an indispensable quality in the accomplishment of results.

Unsettled and wandering ideas invariably lead to decisions whose diversity is their weak-ness.

The man who really and ardently desires to arrive at his goal will mistrust every suggestion that is alien to the main purpose that fills his mind.

The ends he seeks will always be the regu-lators of the decisions he makes.

He will not lose sight of the fact that the effort of will-power that causes him to make a certain decision is for him merely a transitory state of mind.

In order that this state of mind may become definitely established it is necessary that it should produce acts which will tend toward the accomplishment of his purpose.

In those cases in which the action has been prematurely undertaken he must not allow himself to be haunted by any thoughts inimical to the successful outcome of what he has determined to do.

We are now speaking only, it should be understood, of those cases in which such thoughts might turn him aside or lead him astray from his goal.

In all other cases every change of place, every possible betterment that he thinks of should be welcomed by him and critically examined with all possible care.

However, before changing his original purpose, it will be well for him to undertake a serious examination of the facts involved, in order to prevent himself from embarking thoughtlessly upon a dangerous course, or, what is a thousand times worse, arriving nowhere in particular.

The man who would possess the gift of perseverance should, before elaborating the plan which is to be perseveringly followed out, do exactly what all prudent travelers do at the time when they are about to set out upon a journey.

They begin by consulting their tastes, and the reasons or the special interests that lead them to choose one country rather than another.

The choice once made they consider their means.

Next they consider the question of the amount of time they are able to devote to the trip.

They then provide themselves with clothes and equipment of all sorts, of which they are likely to stand in need.

This done, they spread out before them the map of the country they propose to visit and carefully plan out their itinerary, allowing for the delays of the journey and the difficulty of making connections, and marking the towns at which they wish to stop and the spots or the localities which they think will be likely to interest them.

Then only do they actually start upon their journey, knowing exactly where they are going, without being exposed to any delay from the occurrence of conditions which will be likely to turn them aside from the route they have chosen.

Those who act otherwise will very likely be delayed in some manner at the very outset.

The danger of missing connections, which

they have not worked out carefully, will keep them in a constant state of anxiety that will deprive them of all freedom to enjoy themselves. Failure to provide themselves with necessaries will cause them continual trouble, and the slenderness of their resources, which may threaten to give out before the end of the journey, may render it necessary for them to cut short their trip long before they intended.

Others again, unable to resist the attraction of places they have seen from a distance, will allow themselves to be drawn from their pre-arranged line of travel to observe these localities at close range.

In this way they will lose a great deal of valuable time and will run the risk of being led entirely astray.

The worst of it is that these apparently attractive places do not always fulfil one's expectations and so one loses time on one's trip without receiving any compensating advantage.

It is under such circumstances that people who lack perseverance, in place of forcing themselves to return to their original plan of travel without again attempting to wander from it, begin to wander about aimlessly, imagining, at each new horizon that confronts them, that they have made a marvelous find because of the enchanting colors in which distance clothes it to their eyes.

Others, endowed with a less vivid imagination, will travel forward quite regardless of these tempting mirages, but will give up in despair when they encounter the slightest obstacle.

The least fatigue tires them out completely, and they are at once ready to return home and to give up the project whose execution seems to them to be a matter involving altogether too great a complexity of effort.

It may be said with perfect truth of such people that, when they reach home, they will find similar causes for discouragement in the accomplishment of little every-day acts, the doing of which they will put off as long as they possibly can.

The man who is always able to make excuses for himself will by so doing deprive himself of the power that hope will give him in his next endeavor to succeed.

The will to persevere must be the center around which revolve all the qualities that are needed for the conquest of this virtue.

It most certainly is a virtue. The word is

by no means too strong a one, since, well understood, perseverance is made up of the combination of a thousand qualities that we have been taught to admire.

Let us hasten to add that these qualities, in the struggle for life, are, as occasion demands, both weapons of offense and arms for defense.

They serve us to combat all the faults that are the enemies of sincerity and of success.

They attack these faults, batter down breaches in their defenses, and keep on the fight against them until they are destroyed root and branch.

They also constitute the shield that protects us from the mortal wounds that are aimed at our fairest hopes by the faults which hinder us from the practise of perseverance.

These enemies are, to cite only those of first importance:

Laziness;

Discouragement;

Lack of confidence in one's own abilities;

Impatience;

Superficiality.

Laziness, by implanting in our minds the hatred of effort, allows us to succeed only in the very easiest of tasks, those which call neither for concentration of mind nor for sustained attention, and least of all for continuous work.

At this point it may be well to remind ourselves that all enterprises which ask from us a minimum of effort and involve a minimum of complex thought, are almost invariably of second-rate merit.

The ease with which they can be performed by placing them within the capacity of every one, puts them outside of the domain reserved for more legitimate ambitions.

They are attempted and carried out by so many people, that, aside from the laws of supply and demand, they lose all the moral and physical interest that might possibly have been attached to them originally.

The very people who are attracted by them, and drawn into them because they are free from serious difficulty, do not hesitate to abandon them finally when the keenness of competition caused by the large number of people engaged upon such enterprises makes it necessary for them to exert those qualities of action and of perseverance which their laziness absolutely prohibits them from developing.

Lazy people are, therefore, eternally condemned to the performance of second-rate work and to employment which offers no future. Laziness always results in lack of moral tone which tends to keep its victim at a distance from everything which could possibly be given the name of work.

The field of experience is thus allowed to remain fallow, altho a little activity would soon cause it to blossom with the flowers of wisdom, whose perfume would sweeten the lives of the workers.

In the land represented by the mental state of the idle, the choking ivy and a hundred other parasitic plants will soon become completely masters of a territory that no one disputes with them.

It is for this reason that people who are the victims of laziness are endowed with merely negative qualities.

Those which tend to success do not stay with them very long. They die quickly or drag along in a sort of half-dead existence, choked by the growth of innumerable faults, all springing from the one primary defect.

These people soon become themselves exactly like these morbid growths, which do not seem to be animated by any real and vital principle.

Laziness, when indulged in to extremes, always leads to degeneracy in the individual concerned.

It is a well-known fact that organs whose regular functions are habitually supprest ultimately become atrophied.

There are very few people who can use their left hands as easily and well as they can their right hands.

Nevertheless, at the time of their birth, these two members were equally adapted for the same purposes.

But nature has decreed that children shall be corrected the moment they try to do anything with their left hands, for which reason this hand never acquires the skill and the dexterity of the right.

This is so true that those whose occupation necessitates the use of their left hands, such as violinists or pianists, acquire a degree of dexterity in that hand that will always be unknown to those who have not taken special exercises to render the left hand expert.

Next to laziness comes *discouragement,* which is the cessation of all will-power as far as laboring to a definite end is concerned.

The encountering of an unexpected obstacle is always a cause of discouragement.

Virile spirits will see in such an obstacle nothing less than a stimulus and the fascination of the struggle will incite them to persevere on the path that will lead them to success.

But people of wavering courage lose heart with every single reverse whose tendency it is to retard the accomplishment of their aims.

In the face of opposing events they are like the miner who sees huge blocks of stone constantly falling down into the gully he is cutting, and threatening to block the way.

The man who is endowed with perseverance, after deploring such a succession of adverse occurrences, will soon regain his courage by the mere reflection that such regrets are useless and unnecessary.

He will simply make the effort of will required to overcome the piled-up obstacles in his way, and will be all the more rejoiced, when he has successfully accomplished his work, by the fact that it was so much more arduous than he expected and, for that very reason, so much the more productive of honor to himself for carrying it through.

But the man whose will-power has become atrophied will recoil before this redoubling of difficulties. He will prefer to abandon the enterprise altogether to recommencing a second time the work that he has already done and, while commiserating himself over the fruitlessness of his past efforts, he will retrace his steps, supremely grateful if his balked attempts have not caused such changed conditions as to bar the way to a safe return.

Lack of confidence in oneself is always caused by some past unfortunate experience.

However, in place of allowing oneself to become the prey of this most ignoble fear, it will be far more to the purpose to look back upon one's actions and to make a sincere acknowledgment of one's errors.

One sees every day that setbacks of all sorts are almost invariably produced as the result of lack of reflection, of a too easy discouragement, or by a want of active effort.

We may as well admit at once to ourselves that this last is one of the main reasons for failure.

In speaking of active effort we do not wish to imply that extreme mobility which certain people are inclined to dignify by the name of work.

Really fruitful activity is very seldom noisy.

It has the qualities of perseverance, of which it is an important factor.

Too violent movement never lasts and when it is over it leaves weariness behind it.

Now the cessation of effort always brings with it the arrest of progress, and we know already that everything which does not progress degenerates.

From this it results that fatigue by becoming associated in our minds with our disappointment, tends to destroy in us all the incentive to renew the struggle.

In those cases where people of perseverance see nothing worse than a temporary inconvenience, those who lack confidence in themselves will discover an absolutely insurmountable obstacle.

Instead of redoubling their efforts, they will stop to lament over their troubles, and will declare their attempt quite impossible of ultimate success and will devote themselves to the accomplishment of some merely partial result.

Belief in oneself is a mighty lever, in the hands even of the weakest.

In every sort of enterprise, it is the lighthouse which illuminates the road, and gives us the means of keeping the straight path to success, without once wandering to right or left.

For this reason, if one will only take the

trouble to examine oneself sincerely, one will readily recognize that distrust of one's own power can be easily overcome, since it springs from causes that one can oneself determine and that can be altered for the better with very little trouble, with a view to their ultimate suppression for good and all.

The remedy is, therefore, very closely connected with the disease and can be easily found by any one.

As to how it should be applied, all that is called for is discernment and will-power.

Impatience is the exact antithesis of perseverance. It always wishes to hurry along results, and curtails them, even when it does not altogether destroy them.

If procrastination is a deplorable thing too great haste is no less so. It raises insuperable obstacles to all perfection.

How many times does it cut short the development of something, the lack of which spells destruction to the usefulness of the work in hand, which is thus suddenly turned at once from its original direction and its ultimate goal.

Impatient people may be compared to the man who believes he can hurry the appearance upon the scene of a chick by prematurely breaking the shell of the egg that protects it. He thus reduces to nothingness something that, under its original form or under that of the bird that emerges from it, is a source of pleasant nourishment, but that is now of no use to anybody, thanks to his foolish impatience.

Superficiality is the stumbling-block that destroys the efforts of so many people of unequal will-power.

They make trial of all sorts of things, undertake countless tasks, but never fix their minds on a single purpose.

A trifle serves to turn them aside from some task they have begun and leads them to undertake another, which they will abandon with all the docility that is the characteristic of their feeble impulses.

It is absolutely impossible for them to keep themselves in the same condition of mind for any length of time.

Spurred on by curiosity they will turn aside every moment from their projects to rush headlong into others that they will drop soon after with the same chronic changeableness.

Are such people sincere in their desire to do something?

Yes, generally speaking, they are.

But the least little occurrence leads to a change in their ideas. The slightest obstacle, without necessarily frightening them, renders them indifferent and soon disheartens them.

Without attempting to find a way out of it or to combat it in any manner, they fling themselves into some other occupation, the disadvantages of which they do not see on account of their superficial viewpoint.

Their lives are a constant series of new starts and they never reap the fruits of success.

It is fair to say that they never encounter absolute defeat. They never push things far enough for that.

They content themselves with playing with projects, and with constructing combinations, which, without giving rise to much disappointment on their part when they come to nothing, simply remain motionless for a moment and then start off anew like the soap-bubbles that a child blows into the air.

Now let us consider along broad lines what are the qualities of a man of perseverance.

At the head of all these qualities we find one —*tenacity*. Then follow in order:

Composure;

Patience;

Activity;

Poise;

Attention.

There are many other subsidiary qualities, which are not without their own importance, which are grafted on to those enumerated above and give them a great deal of their worth, while playing their rôle of faithful allies.

Of these we will speak in the course of the chapters which are to follow. In these earlier pages, devoted more particularly to the definition of perseverance, we will endeavor to indicate only those elements that are indispensable, and that form the foundations of this master quality that is known by the name of perseverance.

Composure is a quality of the brave.

It is during composure that all good resolutions are made, which lead to profitable achievements.

It is also by virtue of composure alone that one is able to lay down the premises of that reasoning that one finds at the foundation of all enterprises that have in them the potentiality of success.

Without composure no deduction can be thought out that will be in the least worth while,

and it is from such deductions that success
always takes its beginnings.

It is more important than one might think
not to begin one's effort by making a failure
in some undertaking.

Unsuccess is a factor of discouragement for
those spirits which have not been tempered in
the fires of energy, and their discouragement
takes possession of them the more easily for the
reason that they have not in themselves the
strength to fight against events, in which it
pleases them to perceive the workings of a
mysterious and adverse power.

Patience, in prohibiting all indications of
nervousness, imposes upon us continuity as well
as frequency of effort.

But it must be borne in mind that perseverance is nothing else but the will to make this
effort, the reiteration of which makes the continuity.

Patience also enables us to estimate things
under the aspect that they really possess.

It says no to the inrush of considerations of
passion, and, a necessary corollary of these, the
biased judgment of partiality.

It is patience also that enables us to choose
with discernment, and to carry out with clear-

ness and method the actions that reason has counseled us to perform.

Activity is indispensable to the man who wishes to be persevering.

We have spoken already of that false enthusiasm which too often assumes the name of activity, but is nothing more, in reality, than the satisfaction of an exaggerated desire for movement.

Really effective activity does not expend itself in this or that direction.

It never wastes a minute over things that are of no use.

It attempts only those things which, thanks to its power, are susceptible of being brought to a fruitful development.

Division of effort is always the result of activity that has been misdirected.

Many centuries have passed since "Union is strength" was said for the first time, and this maxim, in its journey down to us through the ages, has lost nothing of its truth and of its applicability.

Poise enables us to put to practical purposes the resolutions that we have been able to conceive of during moments of composure, and that patience has permitted us to develop slowly and surely until they were ripe for action.

Poise is the master-quality of those who feel themselves filled with that power of will that inspires bold and brilliant deeds.

It conducts into one channel all the advantages of activity, by permitting it to know its own value and to be utilized in a just cause.

Furthermore, it gives us enough confidence in ourselves to allow free play to the controlling idea in our minds, the counsellor and instigator of our best actions.

Poise must never under any circumstances be confused with effrontery.

It is the quality of people of self-possession, those who seek nowhere but in themselves for the means with which to conquer success.

It allows fancy and reason to act together in the carrying out of resolutions that have been wisely taken, and by moderating the preponderance of impulse in our actions, leaves to reason a place large enough to enable it to assume absolute control when it becomes necessary.

Poise, in giving us confidence in ourselves, enables us to march without a halt toward the far-off goal that our reason has marked out for us.

We are concerned here, it must be remembered, only with a reasoned and considered poise and not with that hardihood of conceit which, having no solid base to build upon, can not long maintain itself in existence and will sooner or later fall to pieces, burying under its ruins those who, for a longer or shorter period, but always one that must inevitably end, have believed themselves able to impose upon others without possessing any real conviction in the worth of their own personal quality.

Attention is the habit of reflection deliberately applied to a certain end.

It is a desire of comprehension, coupled with the wish to apply the teachings that we have received.

Without this quality of attention no enterprise can be conducted to a successful issue.

Thanks to its light, the advantages and the disadvantages of any work we have undertaken will not long remain in the shade.

The lessons learned in the past are, for the devotee of attention sure promises of success in the future.

The blind alone will allow the lessons of life to pass by them unperceived and unappreciated.

Those who are endowed with energy will

strive, on the other hand, to find every possible means for putting the lessons thus acquired into practise.

They will never allow themselves to forget that attention is a powerful factor of success.

It is the parent of experience, which could not exist if one did not use every care to fix in one's mind the details of things, on the faith of which one will begin to build later on.

It is thanks to attention that an inventor is able to make changes in his creations by means of his observations of the defects existing in similar mechanisms.

It is also by virtue of attention that the motive idea can transpose itself into an active force of which the effects will contrive toward the acquisition of perseverance.

We can not make it too clear that it is quite impossible to dream of acquiring this quality if one does not practise the various virtues of which it is made up, while guarding oneself with all possible care from falling into the faults that tend to hinder its development.

It will also be of immense service to us in the formation of those qualities which we only possess in an undeveloped form.

It will comfort us; will make us patient,

courageous, moderate; and will at last lead us to success, by making impossible for us those disappointments and distresses which continually assail, in a greater or less degree, those whose feeble will is not upheld by faith in themselves.

CHAPTER II

THE DANGERS OF OBSTINACY

"EXTREMES meet," declares a proverb whose truth in no way belies the reputation that those ancient sayings have made for themselves.

It is a fact that an excess of perseverance can end in obstinacy.

The militant realities that perseverance transforms into so many motives of realization, become changed, by their defect of obstinacy, into so many utopian dreams, whose unreality is unwittingly—and sometimes even knowingly—defended as fact by those who are not willing to be guided by the counsels of reason.

We are not now speaking of the idealism that knowledge or hard work can bring to fruitage in various ways.

Obstinacy consists in the pursuit of an object when one sees that its successful attainment can not reasonably be hoped for.

The point of departure from this determination to persist in seeing things from the wrong point of view nearly always rests upon a false process of reasoning.

One goes into such an enterprise thoughtlessly, discounting a hope that is dissipated by the clear light of reason like a mist vanishes at the first hint of a sunbeam.

There will often be plenty of time left to change one's determination in such cases, but one becomes entangled by considerations which, in view of the absolute hopelessness of succeeding, must necessarily lose all their value.

Nearly always is there an admixture of vanity in the matter. One does not like to acknowledge that one is wrong and one does not take into account that in persisting in one's error one is aggravating it more and more every moment.

Inertia also plays a part in the wrong-headedness of the obstinate.

To abandon their first attempt in order to undertake another is to their minds merely to double the amount of effort that their will-power has already had so much trouble to call forth.

They do not stop to consider that even the smallest step aside from the direct road is a thing that they must inevitably regret sooner or later, for it leads nowhere and can contribute in no way to the perfection of an enterprise.

The man who is satisfied with his own obstinate folly is like the man who tries to cultivate a field filled with rocks.

All the seed that he confides to the care of the soil will be irremediably lost and, what is far worse, he will also have been wasting his time.

Thus every moment of our lives that we employ in following fruitless ends is part of an hour that we shall never be able to recapture and which, without being of any help to any one, is lost for ever in the gulf of eternity.

But while the man of foolish obstinacy will continue his useless scattering of seeds upon the granite, the man of perseverance, without attempting an enterprise that his reason tells him will come to nothing, will think up some means of making something out of these rocks.

When he has at last hit upon a plan, after carefully weighing all the pros and cons in his mind, he will decide to put his idea into practise, difficulties will not deter him and he will continue with courage and patience the work that he has set himself to do.

A very frequent form of obstinacy is to exaggerate the importance of trifling circumstances and to use them as a pretext for continuing in one's errors.

Sincerity toward oneself can never exist along with obstinacy. Obstinacy delights in clothing things with the shapes that please it and no longer sees them in their true light, but rather in those colors that it wishes them to wear.

This method of conducting oneself can not fail ultimately to lead to the shipwreck of judgment and the complete loss of the power to estimate things at their real value.

It very often happens, moreover, that this wrong-headedness is by no means unconscious. In such cases the lack of consistency in one's reasoning becomes still more apparent and the folly of one's attempts is accentuated.

But one hates to admit that one has made a mistake, and one hardens oneself in one's wrong-doing, so that one can escape confessing that one has recognized its wrongness.

Thus one hopes to be able to deceive others by the act of deceiving oneself.

One argues the case, advancing reasons of which one sees the fatuity. One offers all sorts of obviously insincere arguments and thus deprives oneself of all hope of a return to the path of honesty.

No one is ever the dupe of these wretched expedients, unless it be the person who employs them. Generally in proportion to the unsuccess of his efforts, such a man increases the insincerity of his arguments, until the time arrives when he is quite unable to conceal from anybody the fallacy of his whole point of view.

Another characteristic of obstinacy is the incredulous spirit with which one hears of the success of other people.

The deprest state of mind which is always the result of a failure of any sort causes the growth, in the minds of obstinate people, of a jealousy which always betrays itself by ill-natured remarks regarding those who have achieved the realization of their hopes.

Such people can not, without bitterness, admit the success of others, and they seek by every means in their power to minimize its importance.

Their wounded vanity, coupled with their dread of having to recommence the struggle, deprives them of all kindness of heart or consideration, either for those who have succeeded or for those who have from the start pointed out the obvious illogicality of their own attempts.

Here is another argument that obstinate people fall into quite naturally, and that they consider quite conclusive:

"Oh, yes!" they exclaim. "It is easy enough to characterize as obstinacy an attempt which has resulted in nothing in the end; but if it had been successful you would at once have decorated it with the name of foresight!"

The answer to this is a very simple one:

If this particular attempt had turned out successfully, it would have done so because it was based upon a well-thought-out plan, because it was the outcome of a concentration of thought preceding and making fruitful the resolution that was carried into effect.

All enterprises that are conscientiously undertaken do not, alas, succeed. But those which originate in feverish and ill-considered impulses invariably end disastrously.

"But," the obstinate man will say, "there are people who have made no efforts in that direction and yet for whom everything turns out a success!"

We would not wish to deny that casual good luck does occasionally fall to the lot of people who have made no sort of move toward working for it.

But if one is not satisfied to draw one's deductions merely from a single example, one will see that sooner or later such people will ruin, by their headstrong folly, all the good that has come to them by such a happy accident.

A maxim that one would have to seek far to disprove is that Chance plays a much less important part in life than is generally believed.

The people who achieve success in the world are very rarely indebted for it to this blind deity, and, even if luck seems to follow them continually, one should be able to convince oneself that it is because they have taken every possible means for accomplishing that much-to-be-desired result.

Those who entrench themselves behind these wretched excuses are merely obstinate people who do not wish to take upon their own shoulders all the blame for their own failures and wish to make the world at large responsible for their mistakes.

Should one sympathize with them?

By no means! One should seek to cure them by pointing out to them with all the delicacy at one's command the fallacious lines upon which they have been reasoning.

It would be very undiplomatic to push this point too much. One should at first merely give them a gentle warning, in the form of an opinion that seeks to praise certain parts of what they have tried to do while, without wounding them too much, offering a fair criticism of the weak points in their attempts.

And so, little by little, in seeking with them to rebuild the fallen edifice, one can slip in a bit of good advice here and there under the pretext of helping them to reestablish things on a surer foundation.

Experience will do the rest for them and, if they are at all open to reason, they will soon learn without much difficulty to draw the line of demarcation which separates obstinacy from perseverance.

One must be specially careful not to destroy in the hearts of those people who are sincerely obstinate that quality of hope which was the original cause of their persistence.

On the contrary, it is by leaving this hope untouched that one can accomplish the feat of changing obstinacy into perseverance, since the foundation of this obstinacy was merely a too-blind faith in the future.

One must not forget either that the base of all forms of obstinacy is invariably a false method of reasoning.

The original cause of the trouble must then be eradicated, if one wishes to cure it entirely.

Between obstinacy and perseverance there is simply a difference in the quality of judgment.

The man of perseverance is he whose brain, rendered supple by reflection, never conceives of attempting a project until he has discust it thoroughly with himself and has also talked it over from all points of view with those who are competent to advise him.

He will listen with the greatest care to any objections they may raise, even when they are diametrically opposed to his original convictions, and will make a mental note of every one of them, with the intention of considering them later on and of estimating their value impartially.

If any part of this advice seems to him to be of real worth he will have no false shame about admitting the superiority of the procedure or the line of action recommended.

It is by avoiding obstinacy that one paves the way to success.

The man who is obstinate, on the other hand —and this is the least of his faults—pays no sort of attention to advice, however much to the point it may happen to be.

He listens to none but favorable counsels and turns a deaf ear to all advice that does not harmonize with his own views or join in the chorus of praise that acclaims the undertaking he has in mind or upon which he is already embarked.

He scorns the advice of the old proverb which says:

"The man who listens to only one bell hears only one note!"

He heeds only the flattering music of the bell he himself is ringing.

He stops up his ears so as not to hear the voices of the chimes that would warn him of catastrophes ahead, and even when these have happened, he still stubbornly denies his error, throwing the blame for his unsuccess upon occurrences which have absolutely nothing to do with the events concerned.

One must not fall, however, into the opposite excess and allow oneself to become discouraged at the slightest opposition.

The innate quality of true perseverance, as we have pointed out, is the ability to judge with certainty, which enables us to exactly estimate the value of any argument, and also to appreciate the spirit in which it was offered to us.

Without allowing ourselves to fall into that chronic state of distrust that borders upon the

VIII.4

mania of persecution, it is a very good thing to be able to get the point of view of the envy that suffers from all successes achieved by other people, and will do its utmost to prevent another person from undertaking anything that will be likely to become a source of irritation to its self-love by succeeding.

A very frequent form of obstinacy is that which is familiarly known as the "fixt idea," that is to say the persistence of a single idea that has become so exaggerated that it finally develops into an obsession from which nothing can turn those who have fallen victims to it.

The fixt idea is an exaggerated form of perseverance. It leads in feeble minds to the obstinate domination of an ideal pursued, without leaving any room at all for opposing thoughts.

In the case of fixt ideas, one's whole horizon is confined and closed.

The mind, from constant concentration upon a single line of thought, refuses to take cognizance of any other.

If such a thought does obtrude itself for a moment upon the consciousness, it is immediately banished, or, at the best, with complete disregard of consequences, it is set aside to make room for others that will fall in readily with the dominating idea.

Just as fast as such thoughts occur the man who has become the victim of the fixt idea transforms and makes them over until they become adapted to harmonize with the one controlling obsession that clouds his brain.

Pushed to its utmost limit the fixt idea becomes a monomania.

This state of mind has the essential characteristic of causing every occurrence, whatever its nature may happen to be, to take on the color of the dominant thought that one cultivates so sedulously.

Things which, at the first glance, seem to be absolutely incompatible with this point of view, and quite at variance with the obsession in question, always become a part of it in the end. They become bound to it by threads more or less slender, but which, after a thousand twists and turns, ultimately attach themselves fast to it, thus effecting a heterogeneous jumble of ideas in which the victim of the obsession will always manage in some mysterious way to find a point of contact.

Obsession takes place, generally speaking, at the moment when the obstinacy, pushed to its utmost limits, no longer allows one's physical forces any sort of control over the mental.

It is for this reason that we are witnesses of so many occurrences that leave us lost in wonder.

With the best intentions in the world, there are painters who, because they have been struck dumb some evening by the accentuated violet tones of the twilight, view everything from the standpoint of this color and take to painting violet trees, lilac women, and heliotrope children.

Others, whose sharpened observation has been particularly occupied with form, after having pondered for long upon the circular shape or the regular formation of certain objects, provide us with a school of painting in which right angles and circles riot at will in a manner that is most perplexing to the uninitiated.

Which of us has not been at some time or other a victim of the obsessions that haunt certain specialists?

Dominated by the thought of the disease of which they have made a life study, to the almost complete exclusion of every other thought, many doctors refuse to recognize in their patients the symptoms of any other malady save that which they are in the habit of treating.

Let us add that these doctors and artists are

almost invariably perfectly sincere in their delusions.

We at least are concerned only with such as are wholly sincere. The others, who are all more or less frauds, have nothing akin in them to the obstinate.

They are, on the contrary, very much on the alert to change their mode of operation at the moment when popular appreciation no longer sheds the light of its favor upon it.

We are now considering only the case of those who are obstinate from conviction.

These people, believing that they were proving their perseverance, have by degrees allowed themselves to be drawn to the edge of the declivity that leads first to the fixt idea and later on to complete obsession.

This obsession should be all the more carefully shunned for the very reason that it, in the same way as obstinacy, is the result of a misdirected will to persevere.

It is a most dangerous foe to proper moral balance. At first sight it can quite easily appear to us in the light of a virtue.

The man who has become its victim will be more than disposed to regard himself as a person of great firmness of will, full of the most

earnest determination in the conduct of his
affairs, and a devoted apostle of perseverance.

It is this mistake which, by preventing them
from crushing this tendency as soon as it makes
its appearance, leads feeble-minded people first
into the state of obstinacy, then into the condition characterized by the fixt idea, and
finally into the complete obsession that they in
their folly conceive to be a laudable continuity
of thought.

The remedy for this evil is the reasoned application of healthy perseverance.

Without irritating the victim of such obstinacy, and without making any attempt to persuade him to instantly abandon the object of his
devotion, his thoughts may be directed toward
the desire of realizing some aim which will be
more or less related to his dominant idea.

It will also be a good plan to break the chain
of his obsession by suggesting to him a thought,
not altogether dissociated from it. He will prob-
ably not adopt this thought, but some related
idea, which, with a little patience, one can
gradually cause to take shape in his mind along
the same lines as the obsession that is preying
upon him.

The victim of obstinacy will in this way allow

himself to be led without offering much resistance, as he has no feeling that he is being gradually weaned away from his fixt idea.

This will be the time to substitute for those almost similar lines of thought others of an associated nature, which will give rise in his mind to resolutions that will insensibly tend to draw him away from his original obsession.

One should be careful to choose those projects whose achievement does not involve too long a process of continuous effort.

This is not only one of the principal means of curing obsessions, but it is also a sure way of preventing their recurrence.

It would be a very foolish plan, obviously, to try and demonstrate to a man suffering from obstinacy, and controlled by a fixt idea, that he must absolutely give this up. It is no less ill-advised than to try, in a couple of days, to efface from one's mind some sentiment that has been a controlling factor in one's thoughts for a long period of time.

This attempt, even if it did succeed, would merely have the effect of changing the nature of the obsession, without destroying its hold upon the character.

The obstinate man becomes more and more a

victim to his peculiar form of mania in proportion to his failure to realize his dreams.

Just as soon as he attains his object, the crisis passes.

It is for this reason that it is always advisable to inspire obstinate people with the desire of succeeding along some line which is more or less closely allied to their obsession.

If the idea that controls them is sufficiently comprehensive in its scope to preclude any immediate possibility of realization, one should make it one's business to direct their efforts toward a series of attempts each one of which will be in itself a complete achievement and yet all of which will be dependent upon the dominant idea.

This will give them the impression that they are in no way giving up their pet obsession and for that reason they will offer no resistance to the acts of the person who undertakes to accomplish their cure.

Little by little, their minds, satisfied by these partial achievements, will become less closely enslaved by the main idea, which, in the course of these various different enterprises, will necessarily suffer some degree of modification.

The one important point to be kept in mind

is that the victim of this obstinate obsession must on no account be allowed to discover that one's object is to lead him away from his fixt idea.

If he once divines this he will not only refuse to abandon it, but will become even more firmly attached to it.

The thing to be done is to persuade him that he is following the same object all the time, and it would be the most foolish proceeding to urge him openly to have no more to do with it.

Nevertheless, if this line of treatment is skilfully conducted, the fixity of the idea will become less and less marked.

Without actually ceasing to exist it will become separated into a number of subordinate ideas, which will very soon lead the sufferer from obsession to occupy himself with other trains of thought without knowing that he is doing so.

The smallest results obtained will, every one of them, aid in the splitting up of the dominant idea, and, in a very little while, the great branches of perseverance will burst forth from the unfruitful trunk of obstinacy.

CHAPTER III

HOW TO AVOID EXCESS OF ENTHUSIASM

WE have just proved, in the preceding chapter, that excess is always to be avoided, even when it is in line with the cultivation of a desired quality.

We must never allow ourselves to lose sight of the line of demarcation which separates healthy sentiments from the unreasoning impulses that are inimical to a perfect mental balance.

The moment we attempt to overstep this line, a condition of over-excitement is invariably produced that forces us beyond the limits that reason has set for the harmony that must exist between our thoughts and our actions.

The man who does not pull himself up betimes upon the road of enthusiasm will very soon begin to originate a horde of false ideas which will tend to undermine the power that self-mastery gives to him who has been able to acquire it.

Our judgment will always find itself at fault

upon these occasions, and the resolutions made in the first ardor of an exaggerated enthusiasm will have little chance of enduring.

Having no solid foundation of fact upon which to rest, they will crumble to pieces the moment one attempts to put them into execution.

This would be no great matter for regret, if their disappearance did not always involve the weakening of the feeble effort of will which brought them into being.

The least harmful effect of exaggerated enthusiasm is that it invariably produces disillusionment in its victim.

One pictures the object of one's devotion in such wonderful colors, one arrays it in such magnificent vesture that by slow degrees, and quite apart from one's own volition, it becomes a thing transformed.

The enthusiast is the first dupe of his own imagination.

He is acting in entirely good faith and is absolutely convinced of the truth of what he says, when he enumerates the merits and the advantages of his enthusiasm of the moment. But he quite forgets that the gold with which he is gilding it will very soon peel off.

In point of fact, he will be the very first one to suffer from this unpleasant occurrence.

He has been so honestly carried away by his enthusiasm and his descriptions have rolled up such a veritable snowball of fiction that he does not in the least realize how he is continually magnifying and embellishing his subject, or the changes he has effected in whatever it may be that has had the quality of attracting his fancy.

But when the fever of his passion has spent itself he will be the first to perceive the short-comings of the thing he has been lauding to the skies.

It is rarely indeed that this self-invited disillusionment is not the cause of a very sharp discouragement.

Repeated self-deceptions are frequently the result of too hasty enthusiasms.

In this state of mind, the room left for judgment is so limited that this great regulator of our daily actions finds itself debased to the condition of a mere dependent upon a false partiality that time will always prove to be in the wrong.

Enthusiasm is always the child of impulse and of intuition.

It rejects, just as do the obstinate, all reasoning that can be construed as opposing the schemes that it has formed in the fever of its excited fancy.

Disinterested advisers become for the moment its worst enemies.

It is true that, when the moment of disillusion arrives, the enthusiast will always go back to those same advisers, deploring his own blindness and promising by all his gods to show more foresight in the future.

But on the very next opportunity he will again become the devoted slave of some idea or of some object, whose value or whose beauty he will exaggerate to the limit of his fancy.

The imagination of an enthusiast is as multi-colored as a fairy's robe, but it is also as light and unreal as this imaginary garment.

The moment such a man perceives the real form of the object he has worshiped, divested of the tinsel with which he has adorned it, he throws it aside, lost in wonder at the idea that he could ever have been the ardent devotee of anything so unattractive.

This is indeed the shipwreck of perseverance, for the objects of people's enthusiasm are as numerous as they are transitory.

They are deliberately exaggerated and often completely self-contradictory.

We are not now talking of the things that touch upon the realm of what is called snobbery, and which are as changeable as is that goddess of fancy, fashion.

We are here concerned merely with those exaggerated impulses, which are often of really noble origin, but whose amplification produces a condition of the brain that manifests itself in an exuberance that is difficult to keep within bounds.

It is not the conflagration whose flames dart the highest into the air that lasts the longest.

The fire that lies darkling beneath the ashes may be much less ardent for the moment, but it goes on burning long after the last vestiges of the darting flames have disappeared on the far-off horizon.

One of the main defects of exaggerated enthusiasm is that it breaks the continuity of effort.

When it is too ardent it can not keep long at fever heat.

The impulses of infatuation should be instantly and remorselessly checked.

One should conquer them and reduce them to immediate subjection, just as one does with any foolish caprice.

The visionaries, friends of the unreal, who allow their fancies to carry them far afield from the regions where dwells the rigid truth, are one and all destined to a dangerous, if not to a mortal, downfall.

The stronger the beating wings that have carried them up into this enchanted region, the greater their danger, and the further they have sailed into the realm of fancy the more sudden and the more terrible will be their fall.

But this danger does not concern themselves alone.

If there has been found among them one whose honeyed words have had power to influence the crowd, he becomes a real source of public danger.

It is by just such means that thousands of poor wretches have been led astray, only to pay with their lives for their confidence in these enthusiasts, most of whom were wholly sincere.

How many thousands of them set out with hearts aglow with hope, to discover those lands of gold which, in the end, become for them a veritable land of death.

Are we to assume then that those who have persuaded them to this folly by their speeches are guilty of deception?

No! They themselves were the first dupes.

Their imagination, flattered by the vision of wonderful gains, lit up their belief with its deceiving light, the reflection of which, under the influence of their appeals, glowed in the hearts of their hearers.

They themselves fell victims to the dangerous contagion of the enthusiasm they created and their convictions were real to them.

If, in our enlightened days, the man in the street, who is better informed than in days of yore, lends a less willing ear to these marvelous tales, he is still too often the dupe of politicians, who, armed with a faith that they have elevated into a religion, try to make him believe that they can show him the way to renew the golden age.

How much better it would be to explain to the toiler and to the artizan that hard work and perseverance are the only means by which they can attain to fortune, which never flies from us when we go in search of it armed with these two virtues.

By advocating such truths as this we could entirely prevent the dejection that is always produced by the disillusionment that follows hard upon the heels of false enthusiasm.

It would also put an effective stop to the

disorders which are the inevitable outcome of
labor that has no result.

Those who are really determined upon the
success of the work to which they are devoted
will guard themselves most carefully from too
sudden exaltations.

They will also avoid the excesses of overwork.
Satiety seizes upon those who have not the sense
to measure out the amount of fatigue that they
are able to endure without harm to themselves.

All great results are achieved by sustained
effort and not by occasional spurts. It is by
means of a moderate, but intelligent and regular
amount of toil that men of fame have written
their names on the scroll of posterity.

Nothing is more to be avoided than the tendency to overtax one's strength, as it invariably
involves a period of enforced inactivity.

The fable of the hare and the tortoise will hold
eternally true. It is of no use to run with
speed and to make prodigious leaps, if one
dreams all along the road, or if each dash forward is followed by a long period of rest.

The enthusiast can well be compared with
the hare in the fable.

The tortoise is the man of perseverance, who
does not set out with the idea of beating any

records, but who pursues the even tenor of his way without thinking of anything but the goal at which he aims.

Nothing is less profitable than work which is done by fits and starts.

Disconnected work, performed without the spirit of continuity, never produced results that are satisfactory.

Besides, it tends to make us strangers to that perseverance that one finds to be the base and the foundation of all great achievements.

Unequal efforts, accomplished at first with feverish energy, then abandoned, to be taken up again later on, will achieve the same result as the condition of mind of the craftsman, who, following a new idea every moment, finds his work completely altered from his original conception.

Every piece of work, whether mental or physical, demands an assimilation, a continuity, that can only be obtained by perseverance, which will allow extraneous ideas no opportunity of obtruding themselves upon the mind.

It is indispensable that one should be possest of a single idea in order to accomplish the realization of one's ideals. It is for this reason that we should be distrustful of enthusiasm, because, when it has once shown us our projects in too attractive a light, it will reduce us to utter despair when we see them at length stript of all the fictitious ornaments with which it pleased our fancy to decorate them.

The higher we climb in this decoration the worse the inevitable fall will hurt us, and the time we spend in recovering from our wounds is completely lost to perseverance, unless we use it to make up our minds never again to attempt such impossible ascents.

Enthusiasm is also the avowed enemy of co-ordination.

Once our sense of continuity is at fault, it is impossible to follow out a plan to the end without committing blunders which will hold us back the more hopelessly as we become more eager to complete our task.

Coordination of ideas and of actions is vitally necessary in order to successfully accomplish any enterprise.

If every stage through which the work must be carried is not foreseen and decided upon in advance, if our initial enthusiasm and later discouragement have introduced an annoying disorder in the smoothness of our original plans, there is a very grave probability that the whole affair will result in disastrous failure, if it is not brought altogether to a standstill at once.

Now seriously, what can be expected of a piece of work undertaken in a fever of enthusiasm and then laid aside for a long time?

We must also never neglect the factor of opportunity.

It plays a very important part in every piece of work that is conducted with perseverance.

It is a good thing to carry out any piece of work intelligently, but still better to carry it out at the proper moment.

Opportunity doubles the value of everything.

Now enthusiasm is the avowed enemy of opportunity in that it proceeds by fits and starts.

For the enthusiast there is no such thing as moderation. His must either be the excess of toil or the period of discouragement, in which he ceases altogether to labor, declares himself to be interested in nothing, and professes to have no taste for anything, until the moment when another access of ardor drives him once more to take up his interrupted task.

But what happens then?

This work that has been taken up, abandoned, and taken up again, does not present itself to him any more in its original form.

Moreover, the time that has gone by has modified a thousand details. That which might have passed as a novelty has now become public property, or else the trend of the times has changed and the long-neglected piece of work, in order to have any chances of achieving success, must be completely made over from top to bottom.

The workman is conscious also of other influences.

His energy, that has been changed in direction by his enthusiasms and then brought to nothing by his discouragements, has become unequal and lacks coordination.

But this is not the worst of the affair.

His soul has felt the mastery of the different mental states that have swept over him. His first freshness of impression has gone to join his original ardor, which has become cooled by the chill of discouragement.

His earliest conceptions, not being rendered fertile by the application of perseverance, have deserted him. He has lost faith in himself, and his accomplishments reflect his loss of faith.

If he would persevere at his task he must summon to his aid an energy a hundredfold greater than that of which he originally stood in need.

It may happen that, under the spur of a virile resolution, he can recover once more his first flush of mastery and skill, but he will rarely ever attain to the fulness of his original hopes.

That is given only to the moderate, who, instead of starting by looking at things in too enthusiastic a light, make a compact with reason, the parent of all wisdom and of the restrained conviction that leads one to the perseverance that bears fruit in accomplishment.

Exaggerated enthusiasm is unfortunate for more than one reason.

After having been the cause of I know not how many initial delays, it strikes a deadly blow at hope, that beauteous star whose rays illumine every enterprise of the persevering.

"There is no hope of hoping forever," says an ancient adage.

When we are forced to see the star we trusted suffer eclipse and become lost in clouds of darkness, we finally lose all belief in its light.

Wrong-headed enthusiasts will never admit to themselves that they have carried their lantern too high and at too great a pace through the storm, and that they have neglected to satisfy themselves of the quality of the oil with which it is fed.

They prefer to lay it all to their own ill-luck, and because of their foolishness of heart, Hope, that powerful friend in every sort of undertaking, disappears for ever from the horizon of those who have called upon it too often, when there was no legitimate excuse for its appearance save in the form of a deceiving will-o-the-wisp.

CHAPTER IV

INDECISION THE INVETERATE FOE OF PERSEVERANCE

DECISION is a much rarer virtue than one might suppose. Still rarer are the people who know how to make practical use of this quality.

By the word "decision" we do not mean to imply those sudden resolutions which characterize superficial and headstrong people.

Decision is only fruitful when it is the outcome of reflection and of the habit of coordination, the practise of which enables us to discern very quickly the advantages and the possibilities of any project.

It can never be based upon judgments formed in advance, for, since it draws all its deductions from experience, it is a difficult matter for it to rely exclusively upon antecedent occurrences, inasmuch as events are never brought about in an exactly similar fashion.

Prompt decisions are then formed principally upcn existing conditions, with a due regard to their relative similarity to the facts of the past.

Nevertheless it is the philosophy of these same facts, which, by giving rise to reflection, will bring about the decision which is, in reality, a composite of observation and initiative.

The faculty of being able to collect all one's thoughts and concentrate them is the foundation of a judicious decision.

By practising this mental concentration one very soon learns to neglect no single detail of the circumstances with which we are acquainted that are in the last analogous to those in which we find ourselves.

This study of detail will cause to surge before our eyes a thousand minute observations, which, when taken *en masse,* will constitute proofs of a sufficiently convincing quality to permit of our basing a definite opinion upon them.

This is a point of the greatest importance to those who are desirous of acquiring the virtue of perseverance.

If they do not learn the art of concentration they will never acquire the faculty of observation, and they can never make a decision from an exact knowledge of the facts concerned.

Reflection and concentration are the twin luminaries that shed light upon the dark places of our consciousness.

But how can it be possible to stop and make a decision when there is nothing whatever to indicate in which direction one had better proceed?

The man who has not acquired the art of reflection is like a traveler who finds himself obliged to choose a path in the darkness of night.

Is it not a pardonable thing if he feels a little hesitation before definitely committing himself to a path, of whose direction he knows nothing and whose possible pitfalls he can not see?

This predicament never occurs to those who practise the art of reflection.

The habit they have acquired of weighing carefully the pros and cons of every question, coupled with the facility of concentration they have taught themselves, enables them to rapidly envisage the drawbacks as well as the advantages of the actions that they have determined to carry out.

A few moments of thought suffice them in which to group together the reasons which may lead them to carry out a matter, as well as to review mentally those which may tend to deter them from undertaking it.

Their decision, of whatever nature it may be, will never be a source of regret to them, because it will be founded upon definite deductions, after a careful canvass of all the favorable or unfavorable elements that may effect the success of the enterprise.

This constant practise of reflection will have the further advantage of developing in the man who employs it the spirit of impartiality so necessary to him who wishes, while making reasoned resolutions, to keep them entirely free from even involuntary falsehood.

The people who love to conceal the truth from themselves in order to follow their proclivities, while retaining some semblance of excuse that they can make to their consciences, are by no means so uncommon as one might suppose.

For this reason one can never be sufficiently insistent upon the necessity of exercising absolute sincerity in all our estimates, whether this sincerity wounds our self-love or not, and particularly when it inhibits us from doing something that we should very much like to do.

But decision, in order to become a guiding virtue in our lives, must not only be prompt and based upon firm foundations, it must also be enduring.

Nothing can be more fatal to activity and nothing more of an obstacle to the acquisition of perseverance than the endlessly changing pursuit of new ambitions.

The feeling of inward satisfaction which follows realization will never be known by the man of indecision.

He will never experience the gratification of seeing his work completed, for, long before he has approached half-way toward its completion he will have abandoned it to begin work on something else.

Indecision is often due to an annoying versatility of character which causes one to reject suddenly what one has previously judged to be of value.

This is a tendency toward quick satiety complicated by an unsatisfied yearning for something better.

It is a common but regrettable propensity to be able to see the bad aspects of a thing after it is done and to exaggerate them out of all proportion.

Perfection, alas, is not of this world, and those who seek it run a very big risk of never even catching a glimpse of it.

But people with versatile minds are much less likely to penetrate to the heart of this truth because the hunt for absolute perfection serves them as an excuse for the constant change in their aims.

It is much less humiliating to say, "I have never yet met perfection," than to admit that one has been incapable of discovering it.

This perpetual flux of change enables people of indecision to obtain only an imperfect knowledge of any matter, for the reason that they never take the time to go deeply into anything.

But they never will admit their lack of depth and, since they have scratched the surface of a great many questions, they love to pose before the world as people who are quite disillusioned.

There are two kinds of indecision.

That of which we have just spoken, which is a leading characteristic of people who are incapable of any real achievement.

Such people have hardly began to show interest in a project before they set themselves to discover something amiss with it, with a view to providing themselves with a pretext for no longer following it up.

They welcome with joy all the advice which tends to turn them aside from the path upon which they have been walking, even that which is obviously superficial and partial in its nature.

At the same time they are most careful to

avoid admitting that any advice in favor of the particular project under consideration is as important as it really is.

They are always yearning for new fields to conquer, and seize eagerly upon every occasion that presents itself to them of leaving the work they have in hand in order to commence something else.

If necessity forces them to continue uninterruptedly at the work they have begun they will accomplish it in a perfunctory and half-hearted way.

Their minds are always attracted by work that lies in the future, which they are disposed to begin upon, and in which they discover new advantages every day.

Undecided people of this type are apt to make resolutions that, while relatively rapid, are quite ephemeral in their character.

One desire is scarcely formed in their minds before another presents itself and is welcomed by them with the same fervor.

Their conduct of life is nearly always a succession of contradictions, which are faithful representations of their unstable convictions.

Thus we see them often returning to their original point of departure, and taking up anew

an idea they have once abandoned, only to give
it up a little later, to be once more made trial
of after an interval of time.

Such people will never know the fulness of
satisfaction that floods the hearts of those to
whom it is granted to behold their own completed work.

This versatility is largely due to the superficial way in which their decisions are made.

Since the obstacles have not been given a
moment's thought and their force of will
amounts to nothing, one sees them brought to a
sudden halt by the first obstruction encountered,
without being able to summon up energy enough
either to go over it or around it.

Cowardice when it becomes a question of
making an effort is also a cause of this type of
indecision.

At the very first hint of fatigue the attempt
is abandoned, only to be taken up again after
awhile to be quickly discouraged, and life passes
in abortive attempts, all due to lack of perseverance in following out one's decisions.

There are undecided people of another type:
those who are timid.

These people never have occasion to regret a
resolution that has been hastily formed, for they

surround themselves with every bit of reassurance they can extract from circumstances with the most scrupulous minuteness.

But this exaggerated fear of consequences, coupled with a distrust of themselves that nothing can eradicate, prevents them from ever making the decision called for by the conditions in question.

When they find themselves absolutely compelled to some definite action, they perform it as a rule with timidity which more often than not absolutely precludes the successful outcome of the enterprise.

They wait until the very last moment, then make an attempt to perform the necessary action, but rarely do so with any degree of success, on account of their inhibition by imaginary scruples.

If the undecided people of whom we spoke in the first place are to be blamed for their lack of foresight, these timid creatures sin in the opposite direction by their multiplicity of precautions, which actually prevent them from accomplishing their task.

The one sort do not wish to see the disadvantages of the course which attracts them.

The others see only the bad side of the decisions which they find themselves forced to make.

Superficial people undertake things without due reflection and have to retrace their steps as soon as they become aware of the uncertain nature of the ground upon which they are walking.

The timid, on the other hand, can never make up their minds to start, and, at the moment of departure, some obstacle, real or imagined, bars the way for them, or else the fear of encountering something of the sort affords them occasion for further delay.

The former class are inclined to commence overnight the work that can only be properly undertaken in the morning.

The latter always put things off until to-morrow in order to get out of the way the work which ought to have been done yesterday.

This propensity is an insuperable obstacle to the acquisition of perseverance.

Sins of omission are often more serious in their results than those of commission.

They are certainly less easily to be condoned. One can minimize the importance of a regrettable action, but it is difficult to find pardon for forgetfulness and indifference.

Delays such as we have considered are frequently cultivated by the timid, because their moral development easily accommodates itself to a momentary inaction.

But it would be a mistake to think them satisfied with such a condition, until they have been able to put off to a still later day the decision which they will not be ultimately able to avoid making.

From the very moment when they first postpone the time for preparing this act of will-power, it becomes for them a veritable nightmare from which they are not able to free themselves.

The idea of the resolution that must be taken spoils all their pleasure in the present and the agony is prolonged with each fresh postponement.

It should be added that, during this time, events take their course and the act to be performed becomes charged with additional embarrassments caused by the delay.

It often happens that the opportunity goes by altogether, or that the long hesitation, by making it of no further use, creates a host of misfortunes which it might have prevented.

There are certain physical and moral diseases

in which it is a good thing to resort to the knife.

Indecision, by delaying the operation that will prove the salvation of the person concerned, serves merely to irretrievably compromise the situation.

It is for this reason that we see certain sick people, who have a disease much worse than others, cured by virtue of patience and perseverance in the treatment inaugurated at a favorable moment and faithfully adhered to regardless of the sufferings or the discomfort it provokes.

Others, on the other hand, who seemed much more susceptible of cure, succumb after a long martyrdom that a little decision and some perseverance would have spared them.

Mental disorders often originate in this inertia of will which, by putting off the reforms demanded by the circumstances of the case, allows ruin to become established in a brain, in which a wise decision, backed by perseverance, would have reestablished contentment and peace.

Decision that is prompt and certain is then an incontestable element of success, provided it be maintained without any weakness.

We have already said that, without breaking the rules of prudence, it is easy to make resolutions that are rapid and yet stamped with the hall-mark of wisdom.

First reflection is necessary, then deduction, and finally experience, based upon information we have gathered, all of which will be of immense assistance to us in forming a reliable opinion, that is to say one which has every chance of proving to be so.

One's reasoning can never be infallible or inimitable, and presumptuous indeed would be the man who boasted of never being in the wrong.

But it must be recognized that those people have much less chance of falling into error who have carefully observed the circumstances of the past and have gathered all the lessons of life from the very lips of that teacher without a peer whom we name Experience.

Nevertheless, all this trouble will have been taken in vain if they do not train themselves to give to their decisions the gift of continuity.

In order to come more readily to rapid decisions it is a good thing to prove to oneself one's degree of insight.

To do this one must imagine oneself as being compelled to make certain resolutions, the result of which, however, can be determined, and one must endeavor to decide them in the most

.prompt fashion possible and yet with the greatest degree of wisdom in our power.

One should take as a basis for such decisions the ordinary incidents of one's daily life, making it a rule with oneself never to make a decision except with absolute earnestness.

Then when one is about to make the decision, one should be very particular not to change it, especially when it threatens to have unpleasant results. This condition can, on the contrary, serve us as a very practical lesson.

It will be a proof of our own want of reflection which has dictated the act that we are endeavoring to perform, and we can not fail to draw from it results that will tend to make us much more minutely careful when we are next called upon to render a decision.

This unswerving application to a certain end can be practised with equal advantage with respect to intellectual affairs in exactly the same way as with the daily occurrences of our lives.

If we undertake some task, we must impose upon ourselves the necessity of carrying it out to the very end, whatever its nature may be.

This fixity in following out the objects of our resolutions will be of the greatest service in our every-day life.

Nothing is more likely to lead one astray than the dreams of the irresolute.

One is scarcely ready to undertake something when it becomes necessary, in order to follow their lead, to divert one's attention from the matter in hand to fix it upon some quite alien effort.

If, however, one's protestations are sufficiently vigorous to deter them from persisting in their second project, it is with regret that they will finally abandon it, and they will never cease to grieve over it, in the face of all the evidence against it.

With people of indecision, the ideas that they have given up always appear in the most brilliant colors, while that which they have decided to follow invariably seems to them to be filled with difficulties. They never get all the joy there is out of any pleasure.

Are they about to go out? They regret the comforts of the house. Are they staying in? To go out for a walk appears to them more than attractive and they chafe against the necessity of what they style to themselves an imprisonment.

Life is for them nothing but an uninterrupted series of regrets. They have hardly made up their minds to adopt one decision before they begin to suffer at their inability to act in an exactly opposite manner.

Their intellectual life is as much spoiled by this terrible defect as is their physical existence.

They can not even make up their minds to choose something to read.

They have scarcely begun the work they have decided upon before they begin to regret the one they have previously discarded.

If they decide, after all, to come back to this, they will not fail to find it even more lacking in interest than the one they have abandoned.

This is the pessimistic form of indecision.

The optimistic form is no less dangerous.

Instead of failing to find any good qualities in the things they have or in the resolutions they made, the optimists of indecision see everything through rose-colored glasses. Nevertheless, the things that they give up seem to them none the less attractive.

An old fable recounts how an ass placed between two bundles of hay, each one of which seemed to him as succulent and as tempting as the other, died of hunger from sheer inability to make up his mind which bundle to attack first.

Certain people of indecision are very much like this famous quadruped.

Nothing seems disadvantageous to them in the many different projects they formulate.

They absolutely refuse to see anything but the favorable side of all these schemes when it comes to the point of making their choice.

And, hesitating between one thing and another, many of them allow opportunity to slip by them, an opportunity that is difficult enough to hold at any time and which rarely deigns to return to those who have once failed to grasp it.

It is then indispensable to the comfort of one's life that one should practise the art of being able to make resolutions.

By choosing as the objects of this exercise the events in which we are partakers, we shall have a ready means of controlling them.

It is a good plan to apply ourselves to the decision of difficult questions, as for instance those concerning the people with whom we are associated.

The future will very soon perform for us the office of enlightening us upon the correctness of our estimates.

It is also indispensable that we should concern ourselves only with those facts of which the results can not escape our notice.

It will be obviously useless to become interested in those circumstances of which the main issues are unknown to us, for in such cases we are forced more or less to indulge in prophecy but can not make any prediction based upon knowledge of the facts.

Just as soon as the outcome has demonstrated to us the correctness of our judgment, we shall have no further reason to doubt our own powers in that direction, and decision, the product of serious reflection, will very soon become the basis of all our actions.

The logical nature of our deductions will not allow us to doubt their accuracy for a moment, and we can pursue with perseverance the end we are planning to accomplish, and success will soon come to crown our efforts and to reward us for our conduct of an enterprise that has been so wisely and so courageously undertaken.

PART II
PERSEVERANCE: ITS ACQUISITION AND EFFECT

PRACTICAL EXERCISES

CHAPTER I

HOW TO DEVELOP PERSEVERANCE

LIKE the great majority of virtues which demand a constant effort of will, perseverance is rarely a natural gift.

It may happen, however, that the bent of their characters, the absence of changeableness in their feelings, a certain tendency to reflection, and a predisposition to patience, may dispose some people toward the practise of perseverance.

But they will not make use of this quality with any fruitful results unless they know how to employ it in a rational manner.

The conquest of the art of perseverance calls for two sorts of study.

Mental effort and physical effort.

We will take up the question of the second in the next chapter. Before making any physical preparations for the conquest of perseverance it is a good thing to educate and exercise our minds by the practise of will-power, of self-control, of deduction and of all the other qualities which unite to form the pedestal on which perseverance, the daughter of wisdom and of hope, may be set up.

One of the principal foes of perseverance is the need of dreaming which torments so many people.

There are few, indeed, of us who are wise enough to be contented with our present lot without intermingling with the actualities of our lives some dreams which have no place at all among them.

Such people love to say that they are cherishing an ideal, and use this as a starting-point for transporting themselves into the land of visions.

There is too great a tendency to confound these two conceptions, or rather the two things that they represent.

An ideal is not the dream that can never be realized that certain weak brains love to conjure up, if only to provide themselves with an excuse for carping at life.

Nor is it the vague and unsubstantial speculation in which minds without stability are wont to indulge.

People in this condition, which is familiarly termed a "brain study," like to lose themselves in the contemplation of some more or less abstract idea, the aim of which is generally nebulous and undefined.

They pompously christen this idea "my ideals," and employ it as a refuge for their idleness of mind.

It is, however, indispensable to have an ideal —and this not a vague dream or a chimerical aspiration, but something of the nature of that of which Harold Mansfield speaks:

"The true ideal," he says, "is not a definite goal, which, once attained, leaves the mind inactive.

"It is the continuous impulse toward a desire, which, by means of tangible realizations, gives us the courage to persevere.

"It is the constant effort toward a whole, of which the partial realization provides us with satisfaction and with encouragement."

And, a little later, he defines it thus:

"One may compare the ideal to a chain, of which every link, complete in itself, is added to the one before it to form a durable and constantly lengthening bond."

An ideal is then a dominant aspiration toward which all our acts are directed under the form of successive endeavors, which each and all contribute to its formation.

There is no situation in life, however modest, in which it is not of advantage to have an ideal.

The workman will have thought of becoming the owner of the shop, and he will perform every bit of his labor to that one end.

Does this imply that when the ideal is once attained, it ceases to exist?

Not at all. It merely changes.

Once master of the shop, our workman's ideal will be to make himself distinguished among those who are in the same line of business.

And this same aspiration toward better things, while all the while tending toward a single goal, can find its satisfaction in successive victories, of which every one as it occurs is but a step made in the direction of the end one has in view.

Without becoming actually a chimera, an ideal can approach the realm of fancy as far as concerns the perfection that one wishes to reach.

For certain artists this will be a work of art without a flaw, toward which they continually progress by successive creations.

And for every one of us it will be a goal, whose loftiness, even if it be a little too perfect for us to easily attain, will serve as a refuge against mental deterioration.

Vague dreaming is, then, the enemy of perseverance, to the extent that it blinds us for the moment to our main object, by substituting for it passing fancies and differing goals.

It obstructs the onward progress of perseverance by offering it material of different kinds and often of quite opposing character.

It is the mother of variability, for it leads our minds along all sorts of different roads, and causes us continually to accept and to reject opposing resolutions.

It accustoms the brain to accept this fictitious nourishment, which conceals its hunger but never really satisfies it.

It also disguises truth under all sorts of unreal shapes and sows the seed of disillusionment, which is very near akin to discouragement.

Vague dreaming is, moreover, a great enemy to thought. It is the ivy which rushes to the attack of healthful ideas and very soon chokes them out of existence with its clinging and useless coils.

To know how to think is one of the most favorable conditions for conquering the art of perseverance.

To endow man with the means of thought is to place in his possession the most **powerful of all the instruments** of conquest.

VIII.7

It is by means of thought that we are enabled to apply and to utilize the energies that lie dormant within us. It is entirely by virtue of its strength that we are able to bend matter to our wills. It is also by its help that we can free our souls from the slavery of useless and idle impulses.

It is by thinking in a reasonable way that we are able to draw reliable deductions from the events that we observe.

These will serve as a foundation for what is known as foresight.

We are not now discussing that divination whose occult power is celebrated by certain foolish people, and which they attribute to mysterious agencies.

Foresight is no more than the art of being able to make predictions with practical certainty by basing them upon our observations, which are at once serious, exhaustive, and penetrating.

This is the secret of the success of the self-styled diviners, who formulate their prophesies by basing them upon the most profound study of the subject under consideration.

Many people go into raptures over the wisdom of certain seers, without stopping to reflect that, in the majority of cases, their predictions are no more than the simplest foresight and their divination nothing but observation.

Frankly, what will be one's first thought regarding a person who is anxious to peer into the future?

Most assuredly that he is discontented with the present.

Happy people are more than willing to arrest the march of time and demand nothing of the future, of which they feel no sort of fear.

Here then we have acquired one piece of information.

Next, what does one always ask of fate?

Happiness, of course.

Under what forms?

There are two of these which include all the rest.

First: Good fortune, which embraces glory and fame as well as wealth.

Second: Sentiment, under various personifications.

With a little observation and some experience, one can very soon learn whether the person consulting one belongs in the category of the ambitious or the sentimental.

The age of the person; if a woman, her wear-

ing or not wearing a ring; the nature of the
questions asked; the personal appearance of the
questioner—all these are valuable indications.

The mere sight of dirty shoes, if the weather
has been bad, will indicate straitened circumstances or avarice.

A coat that is polished by use at the elbows
and has shiny cuffs will indicate the worker
in an office—or the better appearance of the
cuffs will show with equal clearness that a pair
of supplementary cuffs have been used to preserve those of the coat.

It is unnecessary to go any further into these
subtleties of observation that certain writers of
detective stories have popularized. We are
simply anxious to prove that foresight can be
exercised quite easily, if it is helped out by the
practise of a minute observation of details.

One talks of miracles when these predictions,
founded upon the most careful deductions, come
to pass, as they nearly always do. One may
be sure that the men who make them are more
than particular not to undeceive their simple-
minded dupes by explaining to them their
methods of procedure.

But if, in place of making this skill in observation the servant of a triumphant charlatanism,

one were to develop it to the advantage of the realities of existence, one could, in the majority of instances, obtain a real success in life by means of the deductive power which has enabled one to foresee what would happen.

In order to exercise this faculty of prevision, it will be a very easy matter to form, after the most patient observation, certain judgments of which we can easily watch the outcome.

It is, of course, undeniable that the most accurate predictions may be brought to naught by one of those accidents which occur spontaneously through the cropping up of some quite unforeseen difficulty.

It is under such circumstances that perseverance comes into play by aiding us to overcome the difficulties occasioned by such occurrences, and by giving us the endurance and the patience that are required in order to be able to combat them effectually.

Perseverance is composed both of a series of definite actions and also of long-deferred expectations, and those last are often much more difficult to endure than actual reverses of fortune.

The man who sets himself to acquire perseverance must arm himself against the impatience that is always born of forced inactivity in the face of opposing circumstances.

There are, however, cases in which the best tactics consist in stirring up a mute energy, ready to proclaim itself the moment the need arrives for it, but strong enough to be able to conceal itself completely, rather than to indulge in unreasonable resistance.

In order to accustom oneself to this storing of latent power, it will be a good thing to cultivate one's will in this particular direction.

To start with, one should exercise oneself by repressing the movements of impatience provoked by delays or similar annoyances.

One should learn to be silent, instead of protesting too vigorously, when one is engaged in an argument. One should impose upon oneself a delay in making any reply, at first of a few minutes duration and longer as one becomes more sure of oneself, and during this period one should strive to suppress every movement indicative of nervousness.

Then, when the time comes to make proof of one's patience, one should apply it, while observing oneself most carefully and endeavoring to overcome all the faults that are likely to interfere with its development.

In order to become persevering, it is indispensable, as we have already said, to have absolute faith in the projects we undertake.

If, for the rest, the enterprise we have in view is based upon sure foundations; if we have studied it sufficiently; if we have been wise enough to draw from similar circumstances the deductions that will enable us to make certain of success in this case; if we are armed with patience and have, in one word, followed all the counsels of perseverance, failure will never be the result of our efforts.

Philosophers claim that all possibilities exist from the moment that we admit the possibility of their existence.

It is impossible to make any better explanation than this of the value of faith in oneself in everything that relates to success.

The idea of any difficulty will be banished at the moment that the firm conviction of succeeding is implanted in our minds. And of all the means of accomplishing this one of the most efficacious is the confidence that one has in one's own abilities.

It would be a piece of childishness to deny the power that lies dormant in words.

Here, then, is a process that one should employ

to fortify oneself in one's resolutions to persevere.

Several times a day, whenever we are able to be alone for a moment or two, we should summon up all our force of will for a few minutes, and then utter these words in a firm voice:

"This thing will succeed!"

When the idea is sufficiently implanted in our minds by repetition, we should add:

". . . because it is impossible for it to fail."

This exercise of fortifying ourselves is a particularly good one to practise in the mornings when we wake.

These words should be the motto of our entire day. With them confidence will penetrate into our minds, inciting us to perseverance in order to achieve the successful attainment of the desired object.

It is no less vitally necessary to fall asleep with the idea of success in our minds.

To this end, before settling down for the night's rest, it will be found a good plan to repeat the phrase of the morning several times to ourselves.

These affirmative and inspiring words will cling in our unconscious memories and will aid us in preparing for the morrow the energies needed for the formation of enduring resolutions.

It must be clearly understood that we are now speaking only of rational enterprises, which fulfil all the conditions of which we spoke at the beginning of this chapter.

If the enterprise of which we are thinking is a visionary one, all our persuasive phrases can only result in regrettable consequences. They will merely contribute to the strengthening and fortifying of the obsession under which we are laboring.

This will afford a good opportunity for commenting upon the philosophical axiom:

"All possibilities exist from the moment that we admit the possibility of their existence."

But we must not suppose that the authors whose books we read do not occasionally commit the folly of seeing possibilities in something which is after all only chimerical.

Theirs is the type of reasoning that emanates from the man who is familiarly known as a "failure," who has made nothing of his career, who has attempted all sorts of schemes without any real value, or who has not had the energy to persevere in a sane and reasonable course.

Such men are always glad to rave at the success of others. They seek to minimize it, if they can not deny it altogether, and even succeed at times in doubting it themselves.

They decry enterprises of real merit, and laud only those which they declare to be of wonderful worth. They make a show of despising really useful efforts in order to employ themselves upon visionary schemes that can never bear fruit.

One thing alone does not arouse the contempt of these curiously warped people. The money that is well earned is never despised by anybody.

It is always the indication and the reward of true success.

We are no longer in the days when it was the accepted thing to find genius languishing on a bed in the hospital.

Talent, in our times, if it is not always rewarded in proportion to its merits, is nevertheless seldom despised.

Inventors get a certain amount of money, greater or less, as the case may be, in exchange for their creations.

Artists can sell their work if they have the gift of pleasing the public.

Musicians play their airs in return for much good currency.

In fact, all those whose talent is recognized can live very comfortably by their gifts or their industry.

There are, it will be said, many persons, who, in spite of the fact that they possess superior qualities, still remain in obscurity, while those who are by no means their equals strut about in the pride and glory of their good fortune.

But why do they remain in obscurity?

Because they are modest, some one will answer.

In that case we shall find it quite impossible to weep over their unsuccess. Modesty should be no part of the equipment of the man who desires to succeed.

When one is thoroughly persuaded with the worth of one's own work one doesn't waste one's time in lamenting.

Those who do this are the timid, who are quite as incapable of making any serious resolutions as they are of accomplishing any act of decision.

They lack faith in themselves . . . they are doubtful of their own ability. . . . Very well! Then why should we believe in them?

If they are so dubious as to their own merits, which they certainly ought to know pretty thoroughly, why should they complain when they see us following suit?

If there is one disease more contagious than another it is certainly mistrust of oneself.

It necessarily involves the entertaining of doubts, since these form themselves so readily, on the subject of the capacity of other people.

From this cause one is only half inclined to believe the man who speaks with assurance of his knowledge or of his skill, when one remembers how much every human being is disposed to judge himself with a partial eye.

How can one have any confidence in the man who, at the outset, acts or speaks in such a fashion as not to conceal from our view the very low esteem that his talents have inspired in his own breast?

It is impossible, when confronted with a too pronounced humility, not to conclude that it is founded upon incurable ineptitude.

It is true that ambition often assumes the external appearance of modesty so as not to antagonize any one.

One clenches one's fists to prevent the arrival in the front rank of a man whose avowed superiority might be considered as a menace to those who are themselves aspiring to such a place, but one allows without fear the passage of the man who, by his attitude of self-effacement, does not seem to have anything in him that may cause him to aspire to become a rival.

There are well-known instances of men who have used this method to arrive at fortune.

Not only have they been permitted to insinuate themselves among the following of this much revered goddess, but often enough among the crowd of her servitors there have been found people who have aided them to gain a place in their ranks in the hope, by this means, of blocking the way for a more dangerous rival.

It is only then that they have raised their heads and shown the world of what they were capable.

The history of our own times records the cases of several men, who, like Brutus, have been careful to conceal their ambitions until the moment when it has become possible to declare them in the hearing of all men.

Such men, too, are among the persevering.

Ought we to blame them or to hold them up as an example to others?

One may rest assured that, since their methods had in them nothing approaching trickery or fraud, they are worthy of our respect in more

ways than one. Of such people it may be said
with truth. "They are a force!"

In the intellectual method to be followed in
the acquisition of perseverance several other
principles are to be observed.

An excellent exercise will be to make it a habit
to examine the means one must employ in order
to undertake with any chance of ultimate success
the initial steps of any particular enterprise.

In performing this exercise in relation to
matters with which we are unfamiliar, so far as
being interested in them is concerned, but with
whose general character we are acquainted, we
can give rein to our spirit of analysis without
any risk, and experience will soon come to our
aid by teaching us some valuable lessons.

Another good piece of advice comes to us from
a Latin philosopher, who said to his disciples:

"Do not let a day pass without some realization, however insignificant it may be."

We can not sufficiently insist upon the fact
that perseverance is always made up of successive efforts. It is a series of acts, of which
each one, taken singly, has no value, but which,
when repeated several times a day, acquire a
power that disconnected and hastily conceived
actions can never possess.

What traveler has not been led to reflect upon the value of perseverance in entering the church of Saint Peter at Rome?

The guide never fails to call to the attention of sightseers who admire the huge statue of Saint Peter, that the bronze of the foot has been worn down at the toes by the lips of the faithful.

Just as certainly as if it had been done with a file, their lips in touching the foot of the apostle have worn it away to an appreciable extent, affording a fine example of the power of repetition.

But will-power can rise superior to reverses and it would be a foolish thing indeed to suppose that, without any repulse, we can reach success, at the very first attempt, in the matter upon which our hearts are set, and without the trial of the moral and physical courage of the daily aspirant by any sort of failure.

Perfection can never be actually attained, and those who pretend that, at the very first trial, they are able to walk without any difficulty along the path of accomplishment, are no more than idle boasters, filled with an exaggerated idea of their own merits, sacrificing everything to their vanity, and disregarding altogether the good impulses that spring from proper pride.

Such people as this will never be really persevering.

In order to become so, they must learn to know themselves better. They must learn to see their own weaknesses clearly and must not exaggerate their own merits.

But by this very act of recognizing both their defects and their virtues, they are furnishing themselves with weapons to combat the former, while at the same time equipping themselves to start upon an expedition of conquest of the qualities that they lack.

So only, thoroughly imbued with the feeling of joy that comes from duty cheerfully accomplished, can they cry out:

"I have done everything in my power to bring this work of mine to a successful conclusion. *It will succeed,* I know, because I *will* to believe so, and *because it is impossible for it to fail!*"

CHAPTER II

PRACTICAL EXERCISES FOR ACQUIR-
ING PERSEVERANCE

"The ascent of a mountain," says an Arab proverb, "is composed of a multitude of efforts, each one represented by the act of carrying forward one foot a few feet ahead of that which sustains us upon the ground."

This amounts to telling us, in that symbolical language that characterizes the Oriental, that no result is obtained except as the consequence of a series of acts destined to accomplish it.

One would laugh, and justly, at the man who proposed to himself to fly at one jump from the bottom to the top of a mountain, but one has nothing but words of encouragement for him who girds up his loins and goes off, supported by his staff, to undertake the climb.

At the same time that it encourages perseverance this proverb condemns isolated effort, however spectacular it may be.

But multiplicity alone will not suffice; there must be joined to it regularity.

111

The writer who produces a page a day, will have at the end of several years a much greater amount of finished work than the man who writes all day for several weeks and then lays aside his labors for months at a time.

But it is not given to every one to be able to perform a certain amount of work day in and day out.

A thousand and one incidents, pleasant or otherwise, will occur to turn one aside from one's daily labor and to put in its place some other task or duty.

At first one merely sets it aside for a little, with the idea of taking it up again immediately, then one is called away by various preoccupations and when one finally returns to the work one has begun so long since, the state of one's mind is no longer the same as it was on the day when one first began it.

The opportunity of accomplishing something worth while no longer seems so apparent to us, and we either become completely disheartened over it or at the best complete it without order or conviction.

This is one of the least of the misfortunes caused by lack of practise in the art of perseverance.

Rare, indeed, are the people who have within them the seeds of patience and of regularity.

None the less, it is possible for every one to acquire these qualities by carefully following out the exercises that we shall now give.

First Exercise.   Count slowly up to a hundred and twenty, observing the time occupied in so doing by means of a watch. This should be about two minutes, to begin with.

If one pronounces the number 120 before the second-hand points exactly to the end of the second minute, one should begin once more, endeavoring so to space the numbers as to insure the right quantity and at the same time the regularity of the interval between them.

Just as soon as one succeeds, without too much difficulty, in arriving at the desired result, one must prolong the exercise by counting 240, then 480.

Certain people can even go as high as 920, that is to say that for twelve minutes they are able to keep their minds absolutely fixt on the single idea of arriving at the point of uttering the number 920 at the exact moment when the hands of the watch record the end of the twelfth minute.

Those who are able to drill themselves into

easily performing this exercise are scholars already well-grounded in perseverance.

Second Exercise. Take a ball of strong twine and, after having unrolled it entirely, entangle the whole in every conceivable way, as conscientiously as you can.

For the first few days no more than a few minutes should be assigned to the work.

It will be unwise to prolong the trial for more than five minutes at the start.

One has to reckon with the nervousness that must necessarily be produced and that too long an application to the task will merely serve to develop.

The exercise will consist then of employing the five minutes in disentangling the tangled mass of cord.

The next day, the interrupted work should be taken up anew, great care being used not to break the twine. We have already said that it must be chosen for its strength, but must not be too heavy.

At the end of a week one can prolong this exercise by several minutes.

After a fortnight, a quarter of an hour may be devoted to it. We need hardly again insist upon the point that the mass of twine must be entangled as conscientiously as possible, and that if one is able to disentangle it before the end of the time set apart for the task, one must, after having wound it into a ball, unwind it and entangle it afresh.

Third Exercise. Put some coffee berries in a small bowl and count them over five times running, to commence with, writing down the total the first time, so as to be sure that you always find it the same.

After a few days the coffee may be replaced by grains of rice, which should be counted in the same way.

In the case where a different total is arrived at, one must begin all over again, entirely disregarding the previous counts.

At the least sign of impatience, stop and take two or three hundred paces at a fairly quick walk, then go back to the work, which must be persisted in until finished.

Fourth Exercise. This exercise, while it affords an excellent lesson in perseverance, will be of great advantage to those who wish to cultivate a musical instrument, because it will help them materially to acquire suppleness of the fingers.

For other people it can not fail to be very

useful, quite outside of the application of which it affords an example, for in teaching them to move their fingers independently of each other, it will tend to overcome the innate awkwardness, and will tend to increase the natural ease of movement of the hand.

The exercise is begun by extending the hand on a flat surface, a table, for instance, then one must endeavor to crook and to extend each finger-joint four or five times, while taking the greatest care that this movement does not involve a similar movement of the neighboring finger.

When one has achieved this result, one can increase the numbe⸴ of these movements, that may be prolonged as high as ten or twenty times running.

This exercise must be performed without hurrying, and with as much regularity as possible.

Fifth Exercise. Place in front of you two glass bowls of the same capacity, one filled with water and the other empty.

By means of a small spoon the water in the first bowl must be transferred to the second, while taking every precaution to spill as little as possible.

These motions must be performed slowly, regularly, and without any sign of impatience.

Sixth Exercise. After having made an estimate of one's muscular powers, one must set
oneself to accomplish the task of raising a weight
greater than one is able to lift at the moment
of commencing this exercise.

One should begin with a weight that one can
handle with some ease, and should practise lift-
ing it for several days, until one is able to do
it readily and without fatigue.

When this result has been achieved a gram
should be added to the weight, and this should
be lifted for two days.

Two days afterward a second gram should be
added to the original weight.

This should be kept up until the point is
reached where the effort involves fatigue.

At the first indication of difficulty, one should
allow the weight to remain at the point reached
and should continue to lift it every day, being
very careful not to change it in the least in any
way.

It must be only at the end of several days,
when the effort is quite readily made, that one
should attempt to increase the amount of the
weight.

This exercise can be repeated in various ways,
to obtain the suppleness or the power of en-

durance one desires, whether in the case of walking, of jumping, or of any other sport.

It is only by measuring out one's physical efforts that one can succeed in accomplishing that of which one definitely hopes to see the fulfilment.

GENERAL OBSERVATIONS

Before commencing these exercises it will be a good thing to prepare oneself for them by taking a few deep breaths.

In order to do this one should stand upright, the chest thrown well forward, the lungs extended outward and the back curved inward.

One should then fill one's lungs to their full capacity and allow the air to escape as slowly as possible.

This exercise is designed to produce composure, by making certain the proper functioning of the lungs and by regularizing the circulation.

Composure is one of the conditions essential to the mastery of perseverance.

Another very important point to observe is never to attempt to overtax one's strength.

Discouragement is the enemy of perseverance, and this is susceptible of a very natural explanation.

All efforts, up to the moment when it becomes impossible to continue them, lead always to weariness, of which the least unpleasant result is that it shows us our goal under disagreeable colors.

The memory of the difficulty we have experienced becomes linked with apprehension of future efforts and retards their performance, until the time arrives when one finds some reasonable pretext for abandoning them altogether.

It is also indispensable, while one is performing these exercises, to fix one's thought steadily upon them and to allow nothing to cause it to wander.

It is for this reason that, at the start, it is essential to attempt nothing that can not be quickly brought to a conclusion, in order to be easily able to retain the mastery of one's thoughts that will prevent the idea from escaping us.

If, in spite of all our efforts, wandering of the mind does take place, it will become necessary to rigidly refuse all indulgence to our own weakness.

The mind should be brought back briskly to the subject under consideration, by redoubling

the effort of attention needed to center it **upon**
that subject.

There is another recommendation of which
the importance must not be overlooked.

It is disastrous for the conquest of perseverance to undertake one piece of work when another is still in process of completion.

We are not speaking here of the different
things which it may become necessary to do in
the course of accomplishing it, and which, far
from doing any injury to it, actually contribute
to the perfection of the work.

We wish merely to describe those undertakings
of a similar nature, of which the beginning of
one must necessarily be an absolute interruption
to the completion of another.

It is quite impossible to stop certain kinds
of work, to commence other tasks of the same
sort without dividing one's energies, that is to
say without doing like the man of whom the
Norwegian fable tells us.

He had to go from a certain place to a certain
other place to rejoin his fiancée. But the direct
road seemed to him a little monotonous, and he
abandoned it to follow a by-path, which he very
soon left in order to try another.

His wanderings became more and more involved, until he completely lost sight of his original objective point. On his journey he wandered from village to village for many long years, without giving any thought, until it was much too late, to his real destination, the hoped-for goal of days long passed.

But his original road was far distant, he had to retrace many weary miles, and found on the way other causes of distraction, so that he did not reach the end of his journey until he had already been wandering over the face of the earth for a very long time.

His sweetheart of former days, left to wait in vain, had cast in her lot with another mate, and the wanderer found himself left alone, poor, and friendless, in the face of an old age which should afford him no place beside the hearth which should have been his.

Those who can not persevere along one single line that will guide them to one particular goal are all like this man.

Work that is frittered away gives one no joy and can never bear any fruit.

To be worth anything, the work of to-day must be joined to that of all the days that have gone before it, which will reinforce it and give it breadth and scope.

The laws of gradually acquired speed are based solely on this one observation.

No machine can be started at full speed.

The series of necessary movements is not produced with the required rapidity and regularity until the preceding movements can be utilized to accelerate that of the present moment.

The propelling force acquired is nothing but the result of past impulses joined to that of the moment, and it will be produced with all its intensity only when nothing happens to interfere with its regularity and precision.

But let a period of rest intervene and the temporary stoppage will lessen this force to a considerable extent.

It is from this simile that we must draw a lesson in our study to acquire perseverance.

To act is a good thing in its way, but to act with judgment is a much better one, and without continuity and regularity no mechanism however perfectly it may be constructed, will give the satisfaction that one expects from it.

It is this precept that we must follow in order to carry out in every detail the exercises of which we have treated in this chapter.

CHAPTER III

PERSEVERANCE IN OUR DAILY LIFE

THE capitalization of energy that is known as perseverance may be put into application not only in the deciding occurrences of our existence, but also in the less important circumstances that make up the duties and the pleasures of our daily life.

Continuity of effort should not be reserved only for great enterprises. To be fruitful, it should be produced just as much in all the actions of the day.

Perseverance, as related to our daily life, can be divided into two categories which are quite distinct from each other.

Perseverance that is obligatory and grudgingly accorded.

Perseverance that is deliberate and voluntary.

The former is a state of submission and is accepted with an ill grace.

The latter is a state of choice.

The one marches in the light, crowned with an aureole of the fires of hope.

The other shirks along in the shadow, limping and grumbling as it goes.

Sometimes it takes heart of grace for a little, and resigns itself to its fate; then starts work in a small way.

It laments no more, but does not indulge in any songs of gladness. It is gray and neutral. It is routine.

We will speak first of the former type. This sheds over everything the light that surrounds it.

At the mere touch of it, the most wobegone objects take on the hues of beauty. It brings joy and happiness to the hearts of those who know it and who practise its precepts.

It is the song of hope, the song that teaches all those who are heavy-laden the belief in a fairer to-morrow, as a reward for the labors of to-day.

With its aid all things become clear and simple.

The faith which always journeys with it revives all drooping energies. The belief in a brighter future, brought into being by its aid, renders less tedious the efforts which we make to reach it.

Finally, our constant advance along the road

on which it guides us, by bringing the goal nearer and making it more real to us every day, gives us the strength to renew the efforts which will enable us to reach it.

"But," some one will say, "how can any other sort of perseverance exist?"

Alas! All those who are compelled to earn their living by obscure toil have to submit to its domination, if only for the moment.

All of us have felt the bitterness produced by the treadmill of enforced habit, as well as that which springs from labor that knows no beauty.

But those who are really persevering very soon throw off this galling yoke.

Instead of going to their daily toil with the melancholy resignation of the ox which plows away for ever at one long furrow, they makeshift to discover some interesting feature about their work and to attach themselves particularly to that.

They have made the discovery that every sort of toil, however humble it may be, has a hidden beauty of its own and deserves a certain consideration beyond that accorded to a punishment inflicted by fate.

However irksome a task may be, it becomes doubly interesting to the man who consecrates himself wholly to it, considering only how perfect he may make it as well as believing in the certainty of some degree of realization.

Is there anything in the world that can be considered more disheartening than to take one's seat every morning in the same drab and unpicturesque surroundings and to pass one's entire day in adding up columns of figures?

Nevertheless many people have found means to render this anonymous occupation an attractive one.

They work their very best and press on toward their goal, seeing in their work, aside from the satisfaction that comes from duty well done, a reward which takes the shape of security and tranquility in the future.

What dreams of pleasant gardens surrounding neat cottages have passed before the eyes of these drudges, clerks and bookkeepers during the long hours of their toil.

They know that these mountains of figures may be the means one day of acquiring such an Eden, and they re-attack their columns of additions with courage, after having acknowledged with a friendly smile the vision of promise that their perseverance will serve to transpose into a delicious reality.

The man who does not know how to practise this virtue may, perhaps, achieve a fair imitation of it by the seeming continuity of his efforts, but since energy and activity are in reality completely lacking, he will end by finding nothing in it but bitterness.

The one feeling he really has is that of weariness.

It must be assumed that his pleasures are few and far apart, because he does nothing to prepare for them.

It is then in a fever of discontent that he performs his daily task.

If it is possible for him to shirk it in any way, he will do so eagerly, but in those cases where he is compelled to perform it in its entirety he will do his work without pleasure, without initiative, and without any idea of bettering his condition.

He will remain for a long while in the ranks marking time, without being able to discover in himself sufficient energy to accomplish the act, or rather the series of acts, that shall carry him forward and disengage him from the crowd.

There is a third type of man, who, bound down by the perseverance of spurious quality that is known as routine, lets day pass after

day, recommencing every morning the work that
he has left the previous evening, laboring without enthusiasm, yet never admitting to himself
that it might be possible not to do this.

His entire existence is a protest against betterment. He fears all improvement as much as he
dreads disaster.

He has the hatred of change.

He is, however, not really satisfied with his
lot. He will tell you frankly that it is not an
enviable one. Yet he will be most careful not
to make the slightest effort to better his condition.

We have spoken so far only of those who
practise perseverance or, at least, who believe
in practising it in wholly different degrees, and
from all sorts of opposing points of view.

There is another class of people whose lot is
still more lamentable than that of the slaves of
routine or those who have to persevere against
their will.

There are those feeble folk who can not find
the courage to accomplish any series of efforts
of any description whatever.

Such people are absolutely foredoomed to be
the victims of an ill fortune whose onward
march they can not check.

If their means enable them to live without active work they will drag out an existence filled with disappointments, for nothing in this world can be obtained without effort, even the things which one gets in exchange for money.

Their unstable wiles will leave them no place for any real satisfaction, and they will abandon every project as soon as they conceive it, always recoiling in fear before the difficulties in the way of accomplishing it.

We must not fail to comprehend the truth of the saying that there is no pleasure to be had without taking pains.

Every sort of amusement demands some continued effort.

Journeys can not be accomplished in comfort until they have been most carefully thought over in advance, in order to avoid the occurrence of a thousand complications, which, by running contrary to our plans, will modify the route we have chosen, or utterly upset our scheme of connections.

The arts all call for a culture that can only be acquired at the cost of great application.

The making of a fortune implies the necessity of sustained labor.

The same holds true in the case of our most

common recreations, such as dancing, or out-
door games, all of which demand a series of pre-
paratory efforts on our part, in order to perfect
ourselves in exercises, which, if poorly performed, represent nothing but weariness that
lacks all interest.

Perseverance is then the guiding virtue of
our daily life.

It is to it, moreover, that we owe the upbuild-
ing or the preservation of our fortunes on the
solid basis of economy.

Every one knows the value and power of
thrift.

Without perseverance it is practically impossible to practise this virtue.

It is designedly that we make use of the word
impossible, because economics are not added up
out of large sums.

One very rarely has occasion to be economical
with thousand franc notes, but one is tempted
twenty times a day to spend a piece of money
of a negligible value, if one considers it as a
single coin, but of considerable importance when
one multiplies it indefinitely.

"The most practical form of economy," says
J. B. Withson, "is not that which deals with
large sums.

"Opportunities for paying out bank notes are relatively rare, whereas we have occasion a hundred times a day for spending small coins, which, taken separately, are certainly insignificant, but nevertheless, when evening comes, form a total that, multiplied by 365, represents at the end of the year quite a respectable sum."

And a little later he adds this judicious advice:

"If we are willing to act in absolute good faith toward ourselves, and will put into the balance the small amount of pleasure that we have received from these little expenditures against the importance of the total sum represented by adding them together, we will have to confess to ourselves that, to use a homely phrase, we 'have not had our money's worth.' "

We do not feel called upon to repeat the many astonishing but withal correct calculations which have been worked out regarding the penny saved every day and laid carefully away.

Nevertheless, it will be very much to our advantage to look around us and to prove to ourselves that the people who practise a wise economy generally end by being able to permit themselves, by virtue of the resources they have accumulated, a good deal more of the comforts of life than do certain prodigal folk who have been infinitely better off right along, monetarily speaking, than they have.

Thus we see that without perseverance it is impossible to economize. Lacking it, the desired goal will always be lost sight of in the urgent need for momentary satisfaction.

When we are able to visualize it once more, we shall be grieved to see that it is still farther off than before, and that our previous efforts have been practically brought to naught by our thoughtlessness of the moment.

Perseverance is also a source of continual joy to those who have learned the feeling of exhilaration that success brings with it.

Successes very seldom come singly.

They are nearly always the result of a number of realizations, all of which have their part in the production of the final achievement.

Moreover the man who knows what each one of these minor successes costs him will feel a real satisfaction in accomplishing them.

One might compare him to a jeweler, devoted to his art, who chisels out with infinite care a quantity of links, which, when taken together, will form a beautiful chain.

He knows very well that these links, when

taken one by one, are worth relatively little, and that it is only their number and their union into a perfect chain that gives them their value.

The magnificent collections that we admire so often have been brought together in a precisely similar way.

One can not help smiling at the inexperience of the man who has the idea that he can get together a collection of this sort in one moment.

It is only by dint of minute and patient research that one is able first of all to find, and finally to assemble together, a number of objects that all belong to the same family.

But what joy one feels when one discovers a rarity, and experiences in watching the increase in number of one's artistic treasures.

Let us hasten to add that in such a case as this art is not the only consideration, and that wealth is very frequently the reward of the patience and tenacity of a collector.

Another form of perseverance that is relative to the affairs of our every-day life is the knowledge of the value of time.

The man who, by the judicious employment of the qualities that go to the making of perseverance, devotes himself whole-heartedly to a piece of work and knows how to concentrate upon it all his thoughts and all his acts, lives with infinitely greater intensity than the man in whose life one attempt follows another continually at more or less frequent intervals.

This can be explained in a simple manner.

It can not be disputed that the time that one gives to an effort that does not last and that inevitably results in a check of some kind should be considered as just so many minutes or hours lost to our lives.

This time, during which one has lived merely to attain a certain object, which is afterward abandoned, can be classed without any further argument in the category of wasted hours, or to express it better, hours in which we have not really lived.

Those are greatly to be commiserated whose lives contain many of these hours.

They are nearly always the prey of melancholy and discouragement. They easily become extremely irritable, and their discontent with themselves exhibits itself in a spirit of quarrelsome contradictoriness that makes them the terror of their families.

The man who is endowed with the gift of perseverance will not become the victim of any such misfortunes.

Filled with the thought of his projects, happy at the partial results which give him the right to envisage a solid success in the future, he marches straight ahead through life, picking the flowers that grow beside his path, never losing his courage, and repeating constantly to himself that this is the only certain means that will enable him ultimately to gather together a magnificent bouquet.

Does this imply that the man who is persevering never makes any mistakes?

People would laugh at us if we attempted to preach such a doctrine.

But these same errors very rarely fail to bear fruit for him. He is wise enough to see wherein he has failed in his performance and to divine the reasons for his failure, and far from allowing himself to become discouraged or from flying off at a tangent, he will profit by these lessons to introduce into his undertakings the modifications that his previous experiences have suggested to him as being likely to lead to success.

In this way he will keep going forward, slowly perhaps, but none the less surely, toward the goal that he has in view.

Perseverance is above all a homely virtue.

It very rarely sees anything worth while in deeds of bravado, which are always deeds of impulse. But does it not require just as much courage to keep up the struggle against the hostile forces that lie dormant in the humble duties of our every-day life as it does to go forth in brave array to battle against an enemy who is visible and in the open?

The courage that works quietly beneath the surface of things is by no means the least meritorious of all, and the devotion which is shown, when it is quite certain to pass unappreciated by any one, is a form of bravery that many fire-eaters are quite unable to exhibit.

Let us consider, finally, what a large factor perseverance may be in producing harmony.

It unites all minds and hearts in one thought which gives them a much greater solidarity than the bonds of blood can ever hope to do.

It endows them with qualities whose powers become gradually manifested in them, by disposing them to the firmness of soul and to the sympathetic kindliness which are the foundations of all familiar and intellectual relationship.

The spirit of continuity, which is always possest by the persevering, leads them to make some good use of everything that is in any way connected with the idea that occupies their minds.

It often happens that they will discover between their dominant idea and a thousand details that appear to be scarcely worth while to other people, an affinity which will be for them the starting-point for the most fortunate developments.

To accomplish this it is merely necessary that one should train oneself first to observe carefully, and then to collect together one's observations upon the subject which, for the moment, absorbs all one's interest.

Our daily life, with its incidents, its joys, its cares, and its duties, that are renewed every morning, is a precious mine of wealth, in which each one of us can dig with the certainty of always discovering something of interest.

Great upheavals occur very rarely; men of genius are few and far between. Therefore, we must not think of waiting for some important event to occur, or for some sudden inspiration to visit us, before we decide to make our resolutions.

In our daily lives such occasions will be replaced easily enough by the minute observation on our part of seemingly insignificant details, that we must take pains to relate—in so far as we are able—to the subject that occupies our minds.

The smallest incident that will serve to introduce into it some additional element, will provide it with a new strength, and will give it one more opportunity of enduring and of obtaining ultimate success.

Stone by stone the most imposing buildings are erected, so also is the humblest cottage.

Therefore, the aim of every one who wishes to acquire the gift of perseverance should be not to let a single day pass by without contributing a stone to add to the projected edifice.

He will soon begin to see it rising, solid and enduring, above the crumbling monuments of superficiality, of laziness, and of want of purpose.

CHAPTER IV

PERSEVERANCE AND THE CHOICE OF A VOCATION

TRUE vocations are, we must admit, very rarely to be found, and the man who is seeking to establish a purpose in life is very often like the traveler who, set down where four roads meet, tries to divine, by means which are as yet quite unknown to him, which of the four is the path he had better take.

It is first of all necessary to state this general proposition: every profession, every employment, presents some advantages and some drawbacks.

The thing to be done is to be able to discuss both the one and the other and, having done so, to weigh them against each other with the desire of being absolutely impartial.

Too many young people allow themselves to be led away by the attractions of the first idea that occurs to them, without making any attempt to examine into it or to investigate its merits.

139

They prefer merely to look upon the bright side of the profession they propose to embrace, leaving its difficulties to be appreciated a little later on.

To the suggestion of others in relation to them they pay no sort of attention, contenting themselves with shrugging their shoulders and replying that every medal has its reverse side.

They set to work at once in their chosen profession and, from the very start, run into difficulties which, in some cases, turn out to be absolutely insurmountable.

They then cherish the dream of retracing their steps, but the difficulties of making a start all reappear in the first years of beginning a new career, and they find themselves in the same unfortunate position as before, which is accentuated by their remorse at having wasted their time.

If they decide to make a third trial of fate, they run the risk of acknowledging their complete inferiority, for, while they are feeling their way blindly, their companions are forging ahead, and they find themselves left so far behind that it becomes a difficult matter to catch up with them without working day and night.

Their task is rendered the harder by the fact

that they must largely increase the amount of work required of them by the profession of their final choice before they can hope even to catch up with those persons who have gone on ahead of them.

It is for this reason that one can not sufficiently impress upon the minds of young people the necessity of profound consideration before making choice of a career.

It will be the part of wisdom to put them on their guard against brilliant mirages, whose glittering reflection too often masks mean and sordid realities.

A really satisfactory choice at the start is the sole means of succeeding in an honorable and enduring fashion.

Have we not famous examples of this guiding instinct which takes hold of the mind, dominates it, makes it the servant of the controlling idea, and renders it capable of performing the most difficult enterprises?

Antiquity has given us the example of Demosthenes, who being dominated by the desire for eloquence, undertook, in order to develop his voice, a veritable battle against the defects that he inherited from nature.

His defective utterance, his clownish gestures,

his weak chest, apparently banished him for
ever from all possibility of participation in
oratorical contests.

But the dominant idea, foundation of all perseverance, upheld him firmly.

Was it perseverance alone that gave him the
strength to overcome his defects in pronuncia-
tion by means of the pebbles that he placed in
his mouth?

Was it not also the enterprise of the dominant
idea which drove him to struggle against the
want of carrying power in his voice by de-
claiming his speeches in the teeth of the wind
and forced him to make his words heard above
the noise of the crashing billows?

He was an exceptionally nervous man, but
nevertheless he determined that he would learn
to repress the impulsive gestures which he made
quite involuntarily. To achieve this he made
use of a means that it took real courage to
employ.

After having carefully studied out his atti-
tudes, so that he familiarized himself thoroughly
with the frequent recurrence of certain gestures, he set a naked sword close beside him in
such a position that the imminence of the
physical danger might put the check upon his

gesticulations that he was not able to impose by the strength of his will.

It would be idle to recount what all the world already knows, and to dwell upon the astonishing results of this heroic perseverance.

But it is of great use to draw inspiration from lessons like these. After having concentrated our thoughts upon ourselves, and having made an exhaustive examination of our tastes, our desires, and our aptitude, so far as we are able to classify them, it may be granted us, by molding ourselves after certain illustrious examples, to persevere upon the road of our choice, and at last to become shining lights in our turn.

There is a story that one day a philosopher, while walking in his garden, noticed some trees of the same species, of which some grew up straight and strong, while others were stunted and withered.

He inquired the reason, and was informed that the first had been planted directly upon the spot in which they were growing, while the others had been transplanted several times.

Turning toward the pupils who accompanied him, he pointed out these trees to them and told them that they ought to look upon them as a symbol.

"Devotion to constantly changing aims," said he, "has for young people the same danger that numerous changes of position have for plants.

"Hardly have the roots had time to form themselves before they are broken by the plant's being plucked out of the ground.

"The same thing holds true for those who abandon the career that they have originally chosen.

"All their former work goes for nothing and they have to form new habits and new aptitudes in surroundings which are little known to them and often full of danger."

It is, therefore, of the greatest importance that we should not start without proper reflection along a road that we do not know, whose difficulties we have not taken the trouble to study, whose pitfalls we are ignorant of, and among whose impassable rocks and dangerous gulfs we may well perish miserably for lack of a little foresight.

In every choice of a profession, whatever its nature may be, two things must first of all be avoided:

Infatuation.

Unreasonable expectations.

We have spoken, at the beginning of this

book, of enthusiasm, and have pointed out how easily it can be turned into wrong channels.

We must repeat this statement in connection with infatuation, which is not altogether the same thing as enthusiasm, but may be considered as closely allied to it.

Enthusiasm generally manifests itself only after we have acquired a certain knowledge of a subject. It is rarely produced solely and entirely by the object that appears to be its cause, and always makes its presence known by outward signs.

If it is not nourished by exterior influences, enthusiasm will very rarely remain at white-heat.

One can then at once predict a disillusionment just as sudden as has been the previous enthusiasm, and which will arrive the more quickly the more ardent the devotion has been.

Infatuation is less expansive. It does not die a natural death for lack of association. It is more tenacious, and more to be feared for the reason that it grows in the same way as enthusiasm.

But it does not die away as the latter does, nor surrender itself easily to abatement, and it conceals itself much more effectually.

While it is relatively easy to moderate the fires of false enthusiasm, it is infinitely more difficult to bring back infatuation into the realm of reality. It goes beyond all bonds of reason and exhibits its lack of perception in every act.

It is infinitely more dangerous, first for the reasons we have already given, and also for its deplorable effect upon the judgment, which it so obscures that one is able to see nothing but the attractive side of the subject in which one is bound up.

The man who demands too much, on the other hand, sees in the course he is advised to adopt nothing but difficulties, drawbacks, and disadvantages.

Of all these he makes a fabric of impossibility, and ends by deciding to reject every project he considers.

If circumstances, nevertheless, compel him to action, the exacting man will be finally forced to make some decision. But he will make it with such an ill grace that it will be almost impossible for him to persevere in it.

His fault will almost immediately transform his work into a burden and his ill humor will develop into smoldering rage.

He will take offense at everything, and will

hold circumstances and his friends responsible for what he calls his "ill luck."

Under such circumstances what part does perseverance play in his new profession?

Alas! At one moment subjected to a whirlwind of exaggerated enthusiasm, at another plunged into an abyss of desolation, it will never succeed in arriving at the point of establishing itself as the prime mover of successful accomplishments.

If one studies the life of any prominent man one will see how valuable a determination to stick to one particular thing can be in the conquest of fame or of fortune. It would perhaps be better to say "of fame *and* of fortune," because, as we have already written and now again repeat, the latter is always the companion of the former.

It may happen that circumstances at the very outset may make it imperative for us to deviate from our choice path, by forcing us to perform courageously a number of actions whose tendency is quite foreign to that which the dominating idea has awakened within us.

But this idea will not disappear, unless one deliberately decides to banish it.

Like a silent and devoted friend, it will follow

us step by step all through our lives, revealing
its continued presence now and then by some
gentle reminder and then withdrawing itself
discreetly to make room for the exigencies of the
moment.

It was in this fashion that the great Goethe
lived for thirty years with the tender spirit of
Marguerite, a reality of his youth that he transformed little by little in his imagination, until
the day came in which, without taking away
from it too much of its personality, he revealed
it to the world in the immortal guise of the
heroine of Faust.

But while these long years were passing by
a mighty thinker took up his place within the
brain of the poet of yesterday.

It is for this reason that in the last part of
Faust, the youthful enthusiasm of its opening
passages changes insensibly into the most profound of metaphysics, the reflection of the
thoughts of the Goethe of a later day.

The dominating idea is never lost sight of,
however. It pervades all parts of the work,
retracing for us the differing phases of the
author's mind, passing from platonic tender-
ness to carnal love, and from the humble
realities of every-day life to flights of fancy,

whose lyricism leads the writer into frequent excursions into the realm of the fantastic.

But whether Marguerite is telling us of her humble tasks or, as in the later portions of the work, the dialog of the great dead on the most exalted planes of philosophy holds our interest, the presentation remains unique, and, thanks to the persistence with which it has been kept before us throughout the years, an immortal masterpiece has been produced.

What is true of things of an exalted type is no less so when it comes down to dealing with the most simple and matter-of-fact realities.

The choice of a profession, however modest it may be, calls forth the same elements of sagacity, of will-power, and of endurance. It demands, moreover, a discernment not only of moral aptitudes but also of physical capacities.

There are physical faults or weaknesses which render certain occupations doubly difficult and we have not all of us the soul of a Demosthenes to be able to combat these difficulties and conquer them.

And further, unless we have hit upon a vocation that draws us irresistibly, we must not forget that the time passed in such struggles is lost to progress.

The effort required to carry us as far as the goal is always a considerable one. Of what use, then, to double it?

We can not too forcibly impress this last point upon the minds of those young people who wish to take up a different profession from that of their father because, as they say, they are too well aware of its difficulties.

But no profession in the world is exempt from these, and for a son to follow his father's profession is to make him a present of the experience that he will not be forced to acquire at his own expense.

If he is dissatisfied with its progress, what is to prevent him from introducing into it all the improvements that modern scientific methods have accomplished in every walk of life.

He will be sure of a quick success, upon the sole condition that, in treading the path that has been traveled by his father, he makes a determination to avoid routine, that obstacle that men of an earlier generation always have a tendency to place across the path that leads to better things.

He must combat this the more actively in proportion to the speed with which he wishes to achieve success, and he will only become successful in this by practising perseverance while abandoning the ruts of habits that afford no glimpse of wider horizons and can never lead to any form of perfection.

CHAPTER V

A KEY TO FORTUNE

It is impossible not to be struck with the power that comes from perseverance when one finds oneself face to face with the monuments of antiquity.

The gigantic sphinxes, which seem to defy the march of time, and which could pass in this world of ours as emblems of the eternal; the pyramids which have resisted the attacks of the elements for so many thousands of years, are above everything else monuments erected by the hand of man to the glory of perseverance.

Think for a moment of the labors involved on the part of men who had nothing but rudimentary means at their disposal in bringing to a successful conclusion these gigantic works which occupied the lives of generations of toilers.

Across the years, through the passing and the reappearing of untold companies of workmen, the dominant idea persisted unmoved, that of

152

leaving to the people who should come after them their monument to the might of a nation.

This is the lesson above all others that should be drawn from this colossal effort so happily realized.

Without a doubt will-power, ingenuity, and endurance all had their part in this work of the Titans.

But all these qualities were mere satellites of the one dominating virtue—perseverance.

Of what use would have been all the toil of a single reign if the Pharaoh who came after had not continued the work of his predecessor?

Before long the scattered blocks of granite, buried under the shifting sands of the desert, would have rejoined in oblivion the ruins of cities, once famous all over the world, but whose very sites are no longer to be traced.

We have established to-day a far different conception of the value of time and of human life.

Our buildings, if they are less durable so far as actual solidity is concerned, are nevertheless less liable to perish than the pyramids.

We no longer rely merely upon huge blocks of stone which are brought together by the superhuman toil of laboring thousands.

Our efforts go farther than this.

Our great achievements are accomplished not by force alone, but by persevering intelligence, that is to say by the assiduity and continuity of labor.

If we no longer leave to our descendants works that bear mute witness to sheer strength toiling in the service of imperial pride, we strive to leave them a reminder of the progress of which our legitimate ambition has been the motive power.

One must not cry out that genius is not within the reach of all the world and that the men are rare indeed who can hope to associate their names with a great work.

There is not one of us who has not a mission to fulfil.

For some of us this may be to preserve intact the names and the fortunes of our ancestors.

By others, and these are by far the most numerous, this fortune has to be acquired.

As far as a name is concerned they can repeat the celebrated phrase of a marshal of the first empire:

"We are our own ancestors!"

That is to say that if our names have never become illustrious it is therefore left to us to give them a luster which shall render them immortal by its fame.

Of this number are the men of science, the inventors—all those, in fact, who, basing their hopes upon the value of reiterated efforts, march steadily onward until they reach the coveted goal.

It may be objected at this point that we are speaking now only of the pick of mankind, and that the great majority of men do not carry within them the ability that could make them famous.

But how frequently we meet men who either through idleness, through carelessness, or through instability of purpose neglect to put to the proper use the gifts with which nature has endowed them.

Have we not all read that the discovery of the law of gravity was due to the fall of an apple, which, one day, became detached from the tree and dropt at the feet of Newton?

Yet this incident has been repeated, through all the centuries, many millions of times every day, and still this common sight had never until then aroused the thought of a single person.

But this little incident, so absolutely ordinary

in itself, produced in the brain of the scientist
a flood of light, due to the influence of the
dominant idea, which, with a rare perseverance,
continually haunted his thoughts.

One of the most striking examples of the
enormous effect of a dominant idea followed out
with dogged tenacity is furnished us by Galileo,
who preserved in the recesses of his brain for
several lustra the idea of the measuring of time,
which was suggested to him when he was only
eighteen years old.

At this period, his attention, already alert,
was attracted by the act of an attendant in the
church at Pisa, who, after having replenished
the lamp of the sanctuary with oil, allowed it to
swing to and fro without disturbing its balance.

It was not until fifty years later that he
actually embodied his persevering meditations
in practical form.

What would have happened if in the impetu-
osity of his eighteenth year he had endeavored
to put into realized form what his observation
had suggested to him?

One might suppose, without being accused of
pessimism, that it would have been impossible
for him at that age to devise a solution as complete as that which he was able to prepare after

long years of study along allied lines and an extended period of pondering over the idea.

To those who are lacking in ordinary courage it will be fair to remark that the perseverance which enables us to accomplish a result, that is to say to realize our dreams, is most frequently due to a series of efforts which at last become a habit.

By this means they lose their difficulty for us, for constant repetition renders them quite easy.

Then with the joy of success there mingles that which is always born of the feeling of duty accomplished and of progress realized.

What more is needed to render agreeable in the present the toil which paves the way for the comfort and peace of the future?

For most of us, perseverance has no other goal but this. It is the means for achieving the success that means a fortune to us, that is to say which ensures the security of our future lives.

Only for a few commonplace minds is fortune merely the satisfaction of avarice.

The ease of soul that comes from the realization of one's ambitions is quite unknown to them.

With the transitory pleasure that comes from possession there is always mingled for them the regret that they have not been able to make more, and the displeasure of not being able to retain intact the treasure that they have so painfully amassed.

Composure, the fruit of hopes crowned by success, is reserved exclusively for those for whom fortune is a means and not an end.

For those whose ambition is limited to the possession of a certain sum of money life becomes devoid of all interest when once this desire is satisfied.

But for the man who desires to become possest of a fortune, not to indulge in idleness, but in order that he may set himself free from the shackles of a poverty which compels him perforce to devote himself to routine duties, the future will enlarge at the moment that his first real success takes place.

Finding himself no longer obliged to labor in order to provide for his daily needs, he can set his face toward the accomplishment of something worth while.

Mastery of himself will be much less difficult to obtain when he is no longer under the necessity of performing tasks in which he takes no interest, nor of undertaking enterprises that gall his spirit.

He can now choose his goal instead of having it thrust upon him by circumstances.

He will have all the leisure he needs for setting in motion or for stopping certain trains of action and, the future being no longer a misery to him, he will be free to practise that latent tenacity which never makes a sign that reveals its presence, but bears fruit without fail in due season.

He will imitate the husbandman who, in the autumn, confides to the earth the grain that shall sleep in it all winter long.

Sleep—no it is not sleep. This is merely the outward seeming. A secret work is going forward in the heart of the grain, which bursts its envelop and allows the precious shoot to spring toward the light.

It is exactly the case of an idea that is not forced to develop instantly under the urge of a feverish haste.

Born in the brain of the man whose perseverance has already gained for him, if not a fortune, at least the certainty of his bread-and-butter, this thought, confided to the care of reflection, will undergo a period of germination the length of which will be proportioned to the beauty of its blossoming.

VIII.11

For the right sort of man, fortune will be not merely the goal of his material satisfaction, but also the lever which will enable him to move a thousand obstacles.

It is not granted to every one to enter life through gates of gold, but each one of us can surely better his position along the lines which seem preferable to him.

Some demand of fate the happiness which seems to them to reside exclusively in the outward advantages of wealth.

Let us leave to carping critics the task of blaming them for it.

Such people are in their way elements which tend to produce the welfare of society as a whole.

By satisfying their pleasures they give to the workers of the world the opportunity to earn their living. Every one of the industries fed by the luxury of the rich keeps alive a swarm of laboring people, for whom the caprices of the wealthy make it possible to take part, in their degree, in the joys of the intellectual life.

It is a well-known fact that those whose work is devoted to producing luxuries for the rich have highly developed artistic tastes.

For the majority of these people their trade is merely the means, while art is the end.

Here is the reason of this. Numbers of the artizans whose work consists in making luxuries of various kinds for the wealthy cherish aspirations of a far higher order than the material toil to which they are constrained by the necessity of earning their livelihood.

It is to the realization of this desire that they apply the surplus means that are derived from the earnings of their daily toil.

It is by working steadily at some material task that most artists have been able to provide the means which they needed in order to create the works of which they dreamed.

It would therefore be unjust, from a social point of view, to condemn those people who see in perseverance nothing but a means of obtaining a fortune of which they appreciate the material advantages.

In the great piece of machinery which we call "society," they are the less vital parts of the mechanism, but are still needed in order that everything should run smoothly.

There are others who ask of money nothing more than that it should fill the rôle of purchaser of good, and seek to acquire it merely to exchange it for wares of much finer worth, the marvels of science and of the mind.

VIII.12

These, too, are also apostles of perseverance. Their will to live finds its nourishment in the manifestation of determination, which is an affirmation of existence.

They know very well that progress of any sort can be produced only by a multitude of realizations that take place before the final goal is reached, and they contemplate with composure the duration of an eternal strife for the conquest of higher things.

To cease fighting is, practically always, to acknowledge that one is beaten.

For some ill-advised people it is to declare themselves satisfied.

But in the heart of the man who is possest by a persevering will, the desire of conquest is never extinguished. Inaction appears to him in the light of a disaster and as a sign of decay.

It must be, in every case, the cessation of all effort in the direction of progress, and the man who does not advance becomes rapidly outdistanced.

For this reason we always notice that those who are inspired by a laudable ambition fortify themselves in their ideal, to the extent of being constantly prepared to transmute their thoughts into acts.

Banishing all irresolution, they will be careful to avoid all sentiments likely to be hostile to their purpose.

They will leave their opponents behind by their tenacity and will disarm them by the continuity of their efforts.

Their quiet and methodical perseverance will result in the triumph of right, and they will impose upon others the authority that self-mastery has conferred upon themselves.

They will be just as well prepared to develop militant energy as mute and latent tenacity, which last quality is much more difficult to practise than the first.

Filled with the dominant idea, which, by the bonds of association, has covered the entire scope of their lives, they will seek eagerly for everything that can serve to extend it, to strengthen it, or to defend it in time of need.

They will repulse with determination all that is opposed to it or tends to alienate them from it.

They will always collect themselves before they act, and will cultivate all the lines of thought that tend to stimulate their energies and to give rise to the controlling acts that make possible the achievement of the tasks that necessity or choice has caused them to undertake.

Those in whom the social spirit dominates the intellectual will learn how to endure repeated rebuffs without discouragement, never forgetting that from these successive defeats must one day spring the final victory.

Appetites and individual interests have no power against the slow operation that changes men's souls and prepares them for a state of life whose ideal approaches as nearly as may be to the good of all.

But none the less must each and every one of them remember never to cease the onward march toward their goal, or rather, toward a series of realizations all subsidiary to the main object in view.

Nevertheless, the more near and the more tangible it becomes, the more will they strive to set it higher, for the moment they find themselves upon the point of obtaining it, their desire for progress will urge them to make it nobler and loftier still.

The life of the people who are really to be envied, whom we may describe with justice as the happy of this world, is above all else composed of successive accomplishments, all tending toward the same end—not actual perfection, for that ceases to exist the moment that we attain to it, since all cessation of progress is opposed to the essential idea of the search for betterment—but toward the desire for perfection, which, like perseverance, is one of the keys by whose aid we can open the gates of fame and fortune.

www.ingramcontent.com/pod-product-compliance
Lightning Source LLC
LaVergne TN
LVHW011912080426
835508LV00007BA/499